The Wonderful Works Of God

By
Bishop Femi Owoyemi

1

The Wonderful Works Of God
Copyright © 2025 by Bishop Femi Owoyemi

ISBN: 978-1-7332330-7-1

All Scripture quotations, unless otherwise indicated, are taken from the Holy Bible: King James Version (KJV) and New King James Version (NKJV).

USA ADDRESS

Bishop Femi Owoyemi
Capstone Ministries Incorporated
241 Webster Avenue Providence, RI 02909
P. O. Box 41235, Providence, RI 02940

DEDICATION
This book is dedicated to the glory of God, the designer and creator of the universe. The mighty God, who endows, empowers, and enables all things to fulfill His purpose. To Him who, by wisdom, power, and might, fulfills the counsel of His own will, be glory forever and ever. Amen.

ACKNOWLEDGEMENT
I would like to acknowledge the patience, selfless sacrifice, and support of my wife, Modupe, in the family and ministry. May the Lord whom you serve continue to richly reward you, in the mighty name of Jesus Christ.

I thank Professor E. C. Osondu (himself an author of many books) who encouraged me to write an account of the wonderful works of God, many of which he witnessed in recent years. I also thank him for the endless editing and revision of the manuscript. May God richly bless your family and the work of your hands in the mighty name of Jesus.

I also thank my daughter, Favor, whose many gifts of grace have blessed the ministry. She designed the front and back cover of this book. The Lord will enrich your gift and make room for you to bless multitudes in the name of Jesus Christ.

3

But these are written that you might believe
that Jesus Christ, is the Son of God;
and that believing you might have life through his name.
John 20:31.

TABLE OF CONTENTS

CHAPTER ONE

INTRODUCTION

Oh, taste and see that the LORD is good;
Blessed is the man who trusts in Him!
Psalms 34:8.

In the course of my journey in Christ and in ministry, I have come to a clear realization that the great and awesome God desires to reveal Himself to people at their level. He wants us to experience Him. Experiencing God fortifies faith. It makes us bold to declare the works of God and puts us in a position to trust Him. Any preaching that does not encourage people to believe that God works miracles, signs, and wonders does not depict God as He is. Over the years, during teaching and preaching, I always shared the testimonies people give of the miracles that God performed in their lives. I do this to inspire faith, gratitude, and confidence in the Lord. Professor E. C. Osondu, who has heard the testimonies over the years and witnessed some of them, compiled a list and encouraged me to write this book.

This book on The Wonderful Works of God will encourage your dependence on the Almighty. It will help your prayer life. You will be confident that God will hear you. It will also help you to be hopeful when the answer to your prayers seems delayed. In the end, you will realize that there is really no delay with God because He makes all things beautiful in His own time, as Ecclesiastes 3:11 says. The book is written to allay your fears and doubts. It will help you rely on God for your miracles. While God is the Almighty, all powerful, all knowing, and everywhere present God, our cooperation with Him is required to enjoy His marvelous goodness. Many people work against themselves because they are ignorant of the principles of God and allow themselves to be deceived into acting against their own interests. Total trust in

God and absolute dependence on Him are central to living a life of wonders. God can never fail. He never lies. He brings about what He says. His promises to us in Scripture are true and dependable. In Isaiah 34:16, He said, *"Seek out of the book of the Lord and read; for none of these will fail nor want her mate. It is My mouth that has commanded it and my Spirit has gathered it."* This means that any promise of God that you encounter in Scripture that is applicable to your situation will be manifested if you believe. The word of God works. It is Spirit and life - John 6:63. It is living and powerful and sharper than any two-edged sword - Hebrews 4:12. It is forever settled in heaven - Psalm 119:89. It is the truth - John 17:17. It will accomplish the purpose for which it is sent - Isaiah 55:10-11. God has magnified His word above all His names - Psalm 138:2. Relying on the word of God is wise because it is productive.

CHAPTER TWO

THE FORETASTE

Call upon Me in the day of trouble;
I will deliver you, and you shall glorify Me."
Psalms 50:15.

I was born in a Muslim home. My father had many wives and many children. He sponsored his children's education only to the elementary school level. After my elementary school, my mother paid for my modern school (equivalent to middle school.) In 1964, at the age of 14, after the completion of my modern school education, I became an apprentice printer at Our Goodwill Services Printers on Aroloya Street in Lagos. I was very good at it, and I mastered all the printing machines except the Heidelberg, which at the time was exclusively used by our foreman, a man named Jimoh.

My monthly stipend of ten shillings was not enough for food, and I went into debt with the food vendor adjacent to the press. It was embarrassing. My colleagues often secured printing jobs on the side to augment their stipends, but I just didn't know how to solicit jobs. I was terrible at marketing. This made me think hard about my future, and I concluded that since it was difficult for me to feed myself, I might not be able to feed my family in the future if I ended up as a printer.

I Called on the Lord

The owner and our master at the press was a Christian convert from the Muslim faith. He made a roster, assigning us passages of Scripture to study and talk about at the weekly Bible study, which he instituted. Whatever your belief did not matter to him. So long as you were his apprentice, you were required to participate. It was at this time that I was introduced to the name of Jesus Christ. In 1965, as I thought about my pathetic situation and gloomy future in the printing trade, I decided to pray in the name of Jesus Christ. My prayer went like this: "God, this printing work cannot be enough for me. I do not know how to get jobs to make money. In the future, when I grow older and marry, I will not be able to feed my family. I want to go back to school. Please help me to do so in the name of Jesus Christ."

My eldest brother, Otunba Lateef Adebayo Owoyemi, was an accountant in the Federal Ministry of Finance. He had returned from England a few years earlier after graduating from Leeds Polytechnic in the United Kingdom as a Cost & Management Accountant, Certified & Corporate Accountant, and a Chartered Secretary. I was so proud of him and always visited him every Sunday. I lived on Princess Street in Lagos but would walk to Morocco Road, Igbobi, Lagos, every Sunday to visit him and his family. On one of those visits, he abruptly asked me, "How old are you?" "15 years," I replied. He asked again, "Will you like to go to school?" I promptly said yes. Then he told me to come to his house early the following Sunday. That day, he took me in his Peugeot 403 LK 4851 car to his alma mater - Ijebu-Ode Grammar School. He spoke to the principal, who agreed to offer me admission. I was overjoyed. I could not believe what had just happened. I was even more eager to see him on Sundays.

Hope Dashed
My hope was dashed on a Sunday not too long after. That day, I met the second wife of my father in his house. My eldest brother's mother was my father's first wife. My own mother was the fourth. My brother told me that he would not be able to pay my fees anymore because my father sent his second wife to recover the loan he took for his education. I went back to Princess Street, dejected and angry, wondering why my father chose that time to demand the loan repayment from my brother. I walked around, dazed and angry.

9

When I visited our hometown a little later, I refused to go to my father's house but instead went to my grandmother's. I even walked past my father but refused to greet him even though I saw him on the balcony. He felt insulted by my rudeness, called me upstairs, and wanted to beat me. But the same woman he sent to collect the loan from my brother was at his side. She pleaded for me and I was let go.

Determination Rewarded

In June 1967, I came home to visit my mother and saw that many of my old classmates in Primary and Modern School were in High School. I decided then that I would not continue my printing apprenticeship but must go to school. My mother gave me ten shillings and told me to return to continue my apprenticeship but I refused. The following day, she increased the money to One Pound and persuaded me to return but I refused. The third day, she told me to return but I told her that I wanted to go back to school and would not continue the apprenticeship any more. She said that she had no money to send me to school and I told her that she would have to feed me, feed my wife when I marry, and also feed my children, because I will do nothing except go back to school. She increased the money to Two Pounds persuading me to return to the printing trade and I told her to apply the Two Pounds towards my tuition.

The Journey Of Education Begins

Knowing that she had lost the battle, she asked me to look for a school. I asked my friend living next door and he told me to speak to one of his teachers who was a native of the town. I arranged a meeting between the man, my mother, and me. At the meeting, he agreed to speak to the Principal of the school to give me admission. I insisted that I would start at the second year. The mid term exams was about six weeks away. The man told me that if I failed the exams, I would be demoted to the first year. I agreed. My mother on hearing

10

that told me that if I failed, she would not pay for one class twice and I agreed. I knew that if I wanted to have an education, I had to pass the midterm exams. Upon admission, I put in all my effort, and God was gracious to me. Not only did I pass the midterm exams, but I came in second overall. Then I knew I was on course. The Lord answered my prayers the first time I prayed in the name of Jesus, even though I was not a Christian. What a marvelous God!

Barrier Removed
I did very well in my studies, always coming out on top of my classmates. In 1969, a year before graduating, my mother could not make enough money to pay my school fees. I was sent out of school many times for late payment of fees. I wrote to my brother for help. He offered to pay half of my fees in my final year and the WASC (West African School Certificate) fee. This was a big relief to me and my mother. My WASC exam results in 1970 were the best in the history of our school. After this, my brother asked me to take a one-year course of study in Science at Ijebu-Ode Grammar School because he wanted me to be an engineer. He paid my fees for that year, but we had a disagreement when I insisted that I would not study engineering in Nigeria but abroad.

Divine Connection
I secured a job with First Bank, then known as Standard Bank of Nigeria. I was a bank teller at their Shagamu branch in Ogun State. Shortly after, a young man named Rufus Okwoli was transferred from Lagos to the bank, and instantly we became good friends. Later, we became roommates. Things worked out perfectly for both of us because Rufus could not cook but enjoyed washing plates, and I hated doing dishes but could cook. So our friendship flourished. Not long after, Rufus secured a Federal Government of Nigeria scholarship to study Accountancy in England. Upon inquiry, he told me about his WASC result, which qualified him for the scholarship. Realizing that my

11

WASC result was better than his, he offered to get me a scholarship form. Prior to this time, my eldest brother, the accountant, visited me at the bank and challenged me for wasting my time working as a bank teller. At the time he said, *"Why can't you do what I have done? Why can't you do it how I did it? Why can't you do it when I did it?"* Remembering those words, I completed the form for a scholarship to study Accountancy. Rufus submitted the form for me. Shortly after, my name was published in the Daily Times newspaper on the list of those offered scholarships by the Federal Government of Nigeria to study Accountancy at South West London College, London. Rufus left for London later that year.

Academic Excellence

I joined my friend Rufus in December 1973 at Mitcham Lane in South London. Early in 1974 we moved into a double room on Thurleigh Road in Clapham South. I started my course in January, and in the November Part 1 exams, I came in 1st and won the Roland Dunkerley Memorial Prize for first place in Part 1. I was listed among the highest-placed candidates in the Institute of Cost and Management Accountants' journal in every exam. I graduated in 1976. The apprentice printer of 1967 who went into debt for food became a professional accountant in 1976. Jesus Christ answers the prayers of those who call on Him!

Career Advancement

After returning to Nigeria in 1978, my career advanced very rapidly. I got a job as Financial Accountant at SmithKline Beecham, now GlaxoSmithKline (1978). Then I was Group Deputy General Manager at Eurotrade Nigeria Limited (1984), Management Consultant at KPMG Nigeria (1986), Managing Director of Rofem Consultants and Finance Company Limited (1988), and Deputy General Manager at First City Merchant Bank, now First City Monument Bank (1992). I was chauffeur-driven by age 30. At age 34, we built

12

our first house. The second house in 1992 was completed in 2001. The Lord did not only answer my prayers for a good education; He also blessed me with a good career and good material possessions.

Voodoo

In 1974 while in London, I had a health issue. A heat wave would well up in me, glaze my skin, and produce terrible and unbearable itching. While speaking, the heat that triggered the itching would start. I kept quiet most of the time and did not answer questions in class. Sometimes I was forced to remove my clothes because of the itching. I wept a lot because the heat and itching were very frequent. My friend and roommate, Rufus Okwoli, was worried and perplexed. When I told my brother about the issue, he asked me to come to Lagos, and I did. I arrived in Lagos in December 1974 after our November 1974 examinations. He arranged with his wife to take me to a herbalist in Shagamu. The herbalist said that I must be initiated into the Ifa oracle (an ancient African divination tool) to resolve my problem.

In London, I bathed with hot water every day. I also ate huge quantities of peanuts. I had the initiation in January 1975 but before then, I noticed that my pores had opened and my body was cooler because I used regular water for my bath while in Nigeria. I did not suffer any itching at all. Though I returned to London with the Ifa, I noticed that by using lukewarm water to bathe and avoiding peanuts, the itching stopped. The hot water and peanuts were responsible for my problem. The Ifa initiation was not the solution, but my change of habit. However, I used the Ifa to pray as I was instructed. On returning to Nigeria after my studies in the UK, I engaged in regular Ifa divination.

CHAPTER THREE

DIVINE ENCOUNTERS

Then He said,"Hear now My words: If there is a prophet among you, I, the LORD, make Myself known to him in a vision; I speak to him in a dream.
Numbers 12:6.

Following my rapid progress, people around me began to encourage me to consult herbalists and voodoo priests more often. They told me that because I was making so much progress, I would die young if I didn't seek protection. The fear of dying young drove me deeper into voodoo practices. Then, in 1992, on my way to the herbalists, I began to have an unusual experience. I would sense that someone was sitting in the passenger seat of my car. Though invisible, I always knew when he came and heard what he said. This invisible visitor always had a dialogue with me like this:

Invisible visitor: "You are very hardworking."

Me: "Yes."

Invisible visitor: "You are very successful."

Me: 'Yes."

Inivisible visitor: "But you have no peace."

Me: No response, because I knew that I had no peace.

Invisible visitor: Give your life to Jesus Christ and you will have peace.

Me: No response because I couldn't see the connection.

I continued my regular and increasing visits to herbalists but my invisible visitor never stopped coming and engaging me in the same dialogue.

Salvation

Later that year, I decided to do what the Lord said. I packed all charms, amulets, ritual soaps, oils, and powders into a sack and threw them into a trash heap. I announced to my family that I had decided to follow Jesus Christ. I got rid of the Ifa and started attending church.

Mother's Salvation

Thy people also shall be all righteous: they shall inherit the land for ever, the branch of my planting, the work of my hands, that I may be glorified. Isaiah 60:21.

I preached Christ to my mother, but she never believed because her father was a Koranic scholar of repute in our town and neighboring towns. After several attempts without success, I found the above Scripture and used it to write a prayer in my journal for my mother in this manner: *"Lord, you said my people shall be all righteous. My mother is my people. I have preached your word to her. I have done what I can do. Only you can give her your righteousness. No one else can. Give her your righteousness as you have said, in the name of Jesus Christ."* I never preached to my mother again but just left the matter in the hands of the Lord.

A few months later, my mother came to visit us in Lagos as she always did. The Friday preceding the Saturday that she was to return home, because I was traveling that day, I made arrangements with my driver to take her back, gave her some money, and bade her goodbye. I expected that she would have gone but was surprised on my return to find her still in Lagos. She welcomed me, beaming with smiles. As soon as I settled down, she came to me, still smiling, and said, "The one you have been speaking to me about came to me in a dream last night and told me that He has given me power. I will go back to tell your uncle (who is the Imam of the community mosque) that I will no longer attend the mosque but will start going to church because I am now a Christian."

"I didn't want to leave without letting you know." Then I asked her, "How did you know Him?" She looked puzzled, and I told her that everyone who sets eyes on Him must recognize Him. Relieved, she smiled more broadly.

Half-Sister's Salvation

I couldn't preach to my half-sister. She was so dedicated to her Muslim faith, and I knew it would cause a rift between us. We were the closest in the family. So I simply bought her a Bible, wrote her name on it, gave it to her, and asked that she use it to pray with the Psalms. Not long after, my half-sister had an encounter in the middle of the night. In a dream, she was asked about her friends who were Christians and instructed to read the second Epistle of John. Being unfamiliar with the Bible, she thought that she heard "second epilepsy of John." After waking up, she decided to pray. She performed the ablution, spread her prayer mat, lifted up her hands, and before she said "Al Akbir" she heard someone say in a loud voice, "Is that what I asked you to do?"

Knowing she was alone in the house with her housekeeper, she went from room to room searching. She woke up her housekeeper, who said that she had heard nothing. Being restless, at daybreak she called her daughter, who was a Christian, and related her experience. Her daughter took her to her pastor, who preached the Gospel to her and she became a Christian. She is very active in the service of the Lord, who used her to build and minister in a church.

Half-brother's Salvation

I visited my half-brother because I was led to minister to him from Hosea 14:5-9. He sternly rejected my ministration and said pointedly, "I will die as a Muslim." Some years later, he told me how he had an encounter with the Lord and became a believer. He enjoys praising and worshiping the Lord.

16

CHAPTER FOUR

DIVINE INSTRUCTIONS AND MIRACLES

If you are willing and obedient, you shall eat the good of
the land; [20] But if you refuse and rebel,
You shall be devoured by the sword";
For the mouth of the LORD has spoken.
Isaiah 1:19-20.

Fraudulent Business Partner Revealed in a Dream

I had a dream that I went into a business partnership with a friend who was not transparent and did not allow me to know what he was doing. I was looking in from outside, trying to see what he was doing but wasn't able to. I had to climb a staircase to get to the window where I could look in. The staircase was rusted and collapsing. After the dream, I knew that I should not go into business with that friend.

Establishment of a Commercial Bank Frustrated

I had totally forgotten the dream not to go into business with my friend when, a few years later, the same friend asked me to partner with him and three others to start a commercial bank. I was excited at the prospects and attended several meetings to facilitate the bank. One afternoon, I left First City Merchant Bank (now First City Monument Bank), where I was a Deputy General Manager, heading to a meeting with my friend and others. On my way, a question came to my mind, saying, "Whose time is this?" I knew at once that I should not be attending a meeting when I should be working for my employer. Then, I was instructed to go back to work, and I did. I did not realize at the time that the Lord was also warning me about partnering with my friend in business because I did not remember the dream at all.

I continued working with my friend on the bank, but he did the bulk of the work. Having made all things ready, we gave the instruction to wire the Fifty Million Naira deposit with

17

our application for a Commercial Banking License to the Central Bank of Nigeria one afternoon. However, that morning, before we could submit our application, the Central Bank of Nigeria issued a bulletin to discontinue accepting applications for banking licenses. The establishment of the bank ceased.

Mortgage Bank Disappointment
Disappointed about our unrealized dream of establishing a commercial bank, and still not remembering my dream of not going into business with my friend, we decided to apply for a Mortgage Banking License. Our application was approved, and we prepared to commence operations. About the same time, my partner experienced a series of carjacking incidents in Lagos and his hometown. I consulted my pastor for prayers. After praying, my pastor told me that the reason my partner had those incidents was that he had been dishonest with me. I dismissed the pastor's words because I couldn't believe that the carjackings had any connection to his dishonesty, as there was no evidence at the time.

I resigned from First City Merchant Bank and assumed duty as the Managing Director of the Mortgage Bank. Within a few weeks of assuming office, I heard that my partner inflated an invoice for the purchase of a diesel generator. My investigation with the supplier confirmed that it was true. He purchased two diesel generators but chose to load the cost onto one generator. The one generator he brought to the bank and the second generator he installed in his house. I confronted my partner with the facts, and he confessed. I was disappointed. I also found that the startup expenses of the mortgage bank that he presented to me were grossly inflated. I prepared the startup financial position of the Mortgage Bank and found that expenses were already 360% of the share capital. I knew at that point that the bank would not survive. I also found out that although all the shareholders paid for their share capital, he didn't. These things confirmed

18

that my pastor was right about his dishonesty, and it was at this point that I remembered the dream that I had!

I was torn between kicking him out of the company or just resigning. Feeling that my friend would be desperate to retain ownership and knowing that the survival of the bank was questionable, I called a board meeting, presented my findings, and submitted my resignation. The mortgage bank collapsed a short time after I left. My friend was arrested by the Banking Tribunal for financial malpractice and held in detention. When I appealed to one of the shareholders, who was his uncle and a retired brigadier, to get him out of detention, he bluntly refused, saying that my partner had almost destroyed his reputation through financial impropriety.

Years later, my partner was involved in other businesses with other partners, but it didn't go well due to his alleged fraudulent activities.

Share Proceeds Donated To Church
Sometime in 1993 after becoming born again, I was reading a book written by Gary Whetstone. It was a powerful testimony of his deliverance and salvation. I then said, "Lord, I just don't want to read about the testimonies of others; I want testimonies of my own. I will do whatever you ask me to do." The Lord then asked, "Will you do what I ask you to do?" I said, "Yes." Then He told me to give the proceeds of the sale of my shares to my pastor. I had put up a number of shares for sale a few days earlier to raise funds for the school fees of my children. So I said, "Lord, the money is for the school fees of my children." I felt that I should not give the money. Then the Lord asked me, "Did you not say that you would do what I ask you to do?" I said, "Yes." Then He said, "That's what I ask you to do."

When I got to my office and asked for the proceeds of my shares, it was a little over Fifty Six Thousand Naira. The

19

school fees of my children were only eighteen thousand Naira. So, I felt I should deduct eighteen thousand Naira and give the balance to the pastor, but there was an eerie silence. I knew then that the Lord was not going to say one more word about it. I also knew that if I did not give the money to the pastor that day, I wouldn't be able to do so. So, I pulled out my checkbook and made out a check for my pastor in the exact amount of the proceeds from the sale of the shares. Leaving work that evening, I went straight to my pastor and handed him the check. When he looked at the check, he started praising God, saying that the Lord told him earlier in the day that He would surprise him that day. As he was dancing, I was not happy at all because I still didn't know where to find money for the school fees of my children. I can't really tell how the school fees were paid, but they were.

House Purchase
Two weeks after giving the pastor the check, I blurted out, "Father, it's been two weeks since I gave the pastor the check. I want to know whether You are the one who told me to give the check or not." A few days later, the pastor told me of a house that was up for sale and said that he wanted me to buy it. I had no money, but I did not tell him. He took me to inspect the house. He also took me to a man at Wema Bank who was the sales agent for the house. We had a discussion with the man and left. A few weeks later, the pastor asked that we go to see the sales agent again at Wema Bank. The man said I was not serious about buying the house. He pulled out a check that he had received for the sale of the house and said that he didn't want to sell the house to the man who gave him the check, but to me. He further said that he even offered to lend me Two Hundred Thousand Naira towards the purchase of the house, and I didn't even respond to him.

I knew the check was genuine because I recognized the name of the person who wrote it. Though I did not recall him ever

20

offering to give me a loan, I apologized and assured him that I would raise the balance of two hundred thousand Naira for the purchase of the house. I took an overdraft facility at my bank of Two Hundred Thousand Naira, using our residential house as collateral. We purchased the house. The Lord gave me a building of four apartments, each 1200 square feet, for four hundred thousand Naira! I repaid the loan that the sales agent gave me within a short time, but the overdraft facility was not liquidated.

Saved From The Spirit Of Death
At a wedding ceremony in Lagos, we learned that our daughter, who was a student at Obafemi Awolowo University, Ile-Ife, had been involved in a motorcycle accident and was rushed to the University Teaching Hospital. My wife and I hurriedly left the wedding and headed to Ile-Ife. We saw our daughter, and the doctors called to inform us of her condition. They told us that our daughter fractured the base of her skull and that she tore the membrane covering her brain causing the brain fluid to leak out through her ear. They said she would not be able to continue her education and that she might not be able to speak again. They also said that to save her life, we must authorize her transfer to the University College Hospital (UCH) at Ibadan.

When I declined the offer and assured them that our daughter would be healed, they accused me of not caring about her. Overnight, the driver and owner of the motorcycle who gave her a ride died, and this gave her doctors greater concern. When we got to the hospital that morning, her doctors insisted that she must be moved to UCH Ibadan but I resisted and told them that the Lord would heal our daughter. The brain fluid continued to leak out of her ear but I was not moved, knowing that the Lord would glorify Himself.

A few days later we came back to Ile-Ife to see her and I sat on an empty bed opposite her. Suddenly I felt life drain out

21

of my body and I slumped on my back. Though still conscious, I could neither move nor speak. I was barely breathing. I saw a video of my life pass before me. No one knew what was happening to me. My wife was busy attending to our daughter. I knew then that I was dying and dying alone. However, I still had my mind functioning. So in my mind, I began saying, "The blood of Jesus" over and over. A while later, sweat broke out all over my body, and I revived. When I told my wife what had happened, she said that I was probably overcome with anxiety, which was not the case at all. In all the situations, I was never anxious, and it was precisely because I wasn't that I confidently told the doctors that the Lord Jesus Christ would heal our daughter.

A few days later, we took our house help along with us to visit our daughter again at the hospital. Our daughter was still in the same room. A few minutes after our arrival, our house help, who was sitting on a chair nearby, suddenly slumped, and her breathing was very shallow. She had never been sick in the years she had been with us. As I began praying frantically for her revival, a nurse took notice and came to my side. After a while, the Lord revived our house help. The nurse, being relieved, then told my wife and I that our house help had experienced a miracle. She said many people who had come into that place healthy had suddenly slumped like she did and died. She was very thankful that the Lord saved our house help. At that time, my wife understood the gravity of what had happened to me days earlier.

A few weeks later, our daughter was discharged from the hospital. I asked her how she felt, and she said she was fine. When we arrived in Lagos, we went to our prayer room to give thanks to God. At that time, our daughter said that since the accident, she had not been able to bend down because of a back injury. We laid hands on her, prayed, and she was healed. Though the doctors said she would not be able to speak or continue her education, she went on to obtain her

22

Master's degree at King's College in England. A few years later, she earned a second Master's degree. She is happily married with two boys. The Lord Jesus Christ made her perfectly whole and did not permit the devil to take her life, my life, or the life of our househelp. Glory be to God.

"Pure Water" Miracle
We established a small bagging plant at the back of our house to produce sachet water - popularly known as Pure Water in Nigeria. The business was doing well. My wife and I were also active in the church at the time. Desiring to see growth in our church, I decided to attend a church growth seminar organized by another church. Immediately after attending the seminar, sales of our pure water ceased. No one came to buy, and our marketing efforts produced nothing. We had thousands of sachet water packs stored on pallets everywhere. We ran out of storage space, materials, and money. We stopped production and began to pray. Our prayers appeared not to be heard because there was no change. Then one night, as I prayed, the Lord told me to put water in a bowl and say, *"This is no longer water. It is the blood of Jesus in Jesus' name,"* sprinkle the blood on the premises, and the stock of pure water. I was hesitant because I had never heard that before. I told my wife, and she said since the Lord told us to do it, we should.

Having filled a bowl with water, my wife, our daughter, and I began to say, "This is no longer water. It is the blood of Jesus in Jesus' name." After a long while, we stopped, and I sprinkled the premises and our stock of pure water. At 3.45 a.m., I finished sprinkling, and before 12 noon the same day, all the stock of pure water was sold for cash. People trooped in as if they had called one another. That same day, customers placed orders for more quantities than we sold.

Driver Healed

We employed a driver as a delivery man for our sachet water business. He was a Muslim. He was very diligent and hardworking. When he did not show up for work for a few days, I sent someone to his house. When I heard that he was sick, I asked that he be brought to me. When he came, he told me that he needed money to buy herbs for his treatment. After I gave him the money, I told him that if he allowed me to pray for him, he would not need to spend the money on herbs. I told him that the reason I did not offer to pray for him before giving him the money was that I didn't want him to think that I didn't want to give him money.

He accepted that I pray for him. My wife, our daughter, and I took him to our prayer room. While praying, as I laid hands on him, he fell. After praying, we left him on the floor in the prayer room. About fifteen minutes later, he came out and told us that while he was on the floor, he saw the vision of the Lord who confirmed to him that he is the Savior. He also said that he had been healed of his sickness.

Kids' Bread Money

Shortly after my salvation, we lost all our resources except our house and cars. Prior to that time, though my wife was a lawyer and even secured a job at one of the banks, we decided that she should focus on raising the children while I worked. I had left First City Merchant Bank and also resigned from my new position as Managing Director of the mortgage bank that I set up with my friend, who turned out to be a fraudulent partner. We relied on funds generated from our sachet water business, which at the time was at its developing stage. My wife and children had embraced my habit of taking snacks. There was a bakery adjacent to our church that baked bread on Sundays. I could not resist the aroma of the freshly baked bread and usually bought several loaves after the church service for my family to snack on.

One Sunday, I had just enough money to buy bread after church. There was nothing in the house, and I thought that the snack would sustain us that afternoon, hoping that clients would come later to purchase sachet water. At the church, I did not put any money in the offering bowl. Customarily, in our church, the offering bowl is passed a second time toward the end of the service so that those who come later may give their offering. As the offering bowl was being passed the second time, the Lord told me to put in the money that I intended to spend on bread. I resisted, saying in my mind that I needed the money for bread because we had nothing in the house. I knew that my children were looking forward to it. Every Sunday, immediately after the service, they come to me with excitement, asking me to buy them bread. It had become a family treat.

After stating my argument and as the offering bowl got nearer, the Lord told me again to put the bread money in. Again, I argued, but when the offering bowl came a second time, I put in the money. Characteristically, immediately after the service, my children rushed to me, asking me to buy them bread. I gently told them that we would not be eating bread that afternoon. I was also occupied with thoughts about how we would find something to eat. We left the church, driving to the house. Suddenly, a car drove past me and frantically motioned for me to stop. As I did, a young man came out of the car and told me that he had gone to the church looking for me and was told that we had just left. He was a member of the church who did not attend the service. He then handed me a bulky envelope and took his leave. I knew the envelope contained money, and I was relieved. Upon getting home, I opened the envelope and found thirty thousand Naira in it. The money I did not want to put in the offering bowl was only fifty Naira! Marvelous are the works of our great and mighty God!

My Mother's Death And Burial

Months before my mother passed away, she told me that I should bring her casket from Lagos in a motorcade to the town for burial. I didn't think much of it at the time. Though she visited us often in Lagos, she lived mainly in our hometown. In December 1996 my wife and I visited her in our hometown. She told us she was a little sick but had recovered. When my wife asked her to accompany us to Lagos, she declined. My wife insisted, and my mother obliged because they were very close. We celebrated Christmas and the New Year. Between Christmas and the New Year, my mother thanked me, always saying that if it had not been for me, she would have suffered neglect. She thanked me and my wife for caring for and educating my nephews and nieces. She explained that she had to bring all of them to live with us in Lagos so that they might escape witchcraft in our hometown. I did not understand the change in my mother. We quarreled a lot because nothing I did ever seemed enough. She always pestered me to give money to people. The list was endless, and I didn't have a relationship with most of them. She always fought me for the money and would not accept any excuses. It was a running battle.

For example, wanting grandchildren, and contrary to my opinion, my mother persuaded my younger brother to marry when he was not financially ready. Not long after, he took a second wife. My brother had three children with his first wife in quick succession, and my mother began struggling to care for them. The second wife left because of suffering. Then my mother, brother, his wife, and the three children moved to Lagos to live with us. I was responsible for their upkeep. I became bitter because I resented having to solve a problem I did not create and about which I had warned without success. My mother believed that I had the financial resources to do what she asked. Her concern was not about what I could do for her but for others. She made no demands for herself, and I didn't understand why I had to care for the people she wanted me to give to.

I was puzzled by her change. It was as if she could not thank me enough. Then she would follow the appreciation with prayers for me. I was suspicious that she was preparing the ground to ask me to give money to people again, but she did not ask me anything. On January 1, 1997 my mother put on a very beautiful attire and went to her church, which was very close to the house. We went to our own church and returned to find many of her church members visiting. They told us that Mama inspired them with her infectious joy, praise, worship, and dance. They named her 'the bride of Jesus' that day. Her pastor also came and spoke of Mama's impact on the members of the church that day. I was full of gratitude to God for the salvation of her soul.

On January 3rd, my wife went to my mother's room on the ground floor, as she always did, to greet her. She later told me that upon entering Mama's room that morning and looking at her, she felt that Mama was thinking her death was near. She assured her that all was well and that she would live, but was surprised by Mama's guarded response. She left for classes because she was studying for her law degree at the time. That day, I went in and out of sleep and did not come downstairs to see my mother. Later in the day, coming back from her class, my wife went to Mama's room and found her unresponsive. She raised an alarm, which brought me to Mama's room. I found my mother unresponsive, and we began to pray. Not long after, she revived, and when I asked her what was the matter, she said all was well.

We brought her out to the patio, made tea for her, and I listened to a cassette tape of a pastor preaching. Suddenly, the Lord spoke to me, saying, "Let her go." I knew my mother would be with the Lord that day. In response to the

27

Lord's words, I asked my mother if she would like to go back to bed, and she said she would. As soon as she got into bed, she returned to the exact state in which we found her before we prayed. She passed away less than thirty minutes later. It was the first time I witnessed the death of a person close to me. I was confused but comforted that she died in the Lord. We took her to the mortuary the following morning.

I had only three hundred Naira when my mother died. Before ever thinking of how to raise money, my neighbor gave me seven thousand Naira without solicitation and said I could pay him back whenever I could. I paid the mortuary expenses of three thousand Naira from the money. I sent one of my nephews who lived with us to inform relatives in our hometown of the passing of my mother.

Confirmation Of Mother's Conversion
My mother was the daughter of a reputable Koranic scholar named Akewusola - meaning a blessed Koranic scholar. His son - my mother's half-brother was the Chief Imam of the town. Under Muslim rites, my mother ought to have been buried the same day or the day following her death. One of my cousins, who was older than I, had questioned why I did not bring my mother's body for burial. I explained that my mother had converted and instructed me to give her a Christian burial. She disagreed, saying, "If my mother had converted to Christianity, she would have told me." She called my mother her mother because, though her aunt, she had helped to raise her. She said that she would make inquiries in the town, and if she found it to be true, she would support me in all that I needed to do for the burial. A few days later, she came to Lagos to inform me that in a dream, my mother appeared to her in a car that had a cross on it to show her that she was a Christian. She also confirmed the testimony of Mama's conversion through many other people in the town.

The Chief Imam Cursed

I knew that I had to speak to the Chief Imam before my mother's burial. I went to our hometown for that purpose, and my cousin, now in support of a Christian burial for my mother, offered to accompany me. Getting there, we found the Chief Imam with his first wife and his own younger sister. He asked me why I did not bring my mother's body for burial according to Muslim rites. I told him that my mother had converted and asked me to give her a Christian burial. He was furious at my audacity to say such a thing and questioned why I wanted to bury the daughter of a reputable Muslim scholar as a Christian. I told him of my mother's instruction, and he began to curse in anger. Finally, he said, "If we have a son who does not want to listen to us, even if he is as high as heaven, we will bring him down." I was not at all disturbed by his curses and threats. I had determined to follow my mother's wishes. Knowing that I would not budge, he let us go. Before we got into the car in front of the Chief Imam's house, my cousin said she was surprised by the curses and threats of the Chief Imam. Then I told her, "If the Chief Imam makes any move to harm me, he would die."

Market Prices Brought Down Overnight

Burial in our part of the world is a huge event. Huge crowd from the town and invitees were entertained. We hired a musicians. Logistical arrangements involved the purchase of foodstuff, drinks, water, drinking cups, hiring cooks, plates, stewards to serve food and drinks, guest parking, ushers to lead guests from car park to the venue, sitting of guests etc. We planned and assigned roles. Many of my friends were on hand to help. We bought two cows and many bags of rice to prepare for guests. The burial was set for Saturday February 15 and we were pleased because things were going well. A few days to the burial, we went to our home town.

The only item not yet purchased were cooking ingredients because we had no place to store them. We decided to wait until the day before the burial. The prices of ingredients suddenly tripled at the market and we did not have enough money to get what we need. So my wife and I prayed asking the Lord to bring down the prices. When we sent people to buy ingredients the following morning, they found that prices had dropped drastically. They got all the ingredients we needed and the following morning, prices shot back up!

Cow Incident

I was speaking to my cousin in front of the house the day before the burial when one of the cows came loose from the stakes and headed in our direction. A cow that had come loose in a similar manner in a nearby town a few days earlier had gored and killed some people. We hurriedly got into the car and took off. The cow ran a considerable distance and went into the forest. A search party was quickly organized, but they could not find the cow that afternoon or all that night. My elder half-brother told me the following morning that since the cow was not found, we would have to manage the other cow for the burial. However, during the night, the Lord showed me in a vision that the cow was being cooked. When I told my half-brother, he was surprised.

Motorcade Into Town

That morning, I went to Lagos to bring my mother's body back to town. To honor her request, we brought her casket in a motorcade from Lagos to our hometown. It was on the way that I remembered that she had told me to bring her body in a motorcade to our hometown for burial. Then it dawned on me that she knew she would die in Lagos. Ordinarily, no one would have thought that she would die in Lagos. It certainly did not occur to me that she would. When we visited her in our hometown, my wife had to pressure her to return with us to Lagos, not knowing that she was being used to fulfill her desire! This was amazing to me because my mother spent more time in our hometown than in Lagos.

We arrived in town as St. Peter's Primary School celebrated winning the finals of a soccer tournament. They carried their trophy, went in front of our motorcade singing and dancing. As if they won the trophy for my mother, they led us to where my mother was to lie in state.

Before coming back from Lagos, the cow that ran off was found, killed, and cooked as the Lord revealed overnight.

Miraculous Provisions

The Lord made provisions for my mother's burial. We had all that we needed and did not borrow. I paid the seven thousand Naira lent to me by my neighbor within a few days. As we were packing up at the event venue, one of my friends with a loud voice said, "Femi Owoyemi, you have buried your mother gloriously without borrowing from any one!" We all laughed. However, the Lord glorified himself through his words. We had spent five hundred thousand Naira on the burial without having to borrow. God is wonderful!

The Chief Imam Died Suddenly

My cousin who accompanied me to see the chief Imam came to Lagos less than two months after my mother's burial. She was visibly shaken and said, "You said so, the chief Imam has died. He was conducting a service about half a mile from his house when he suddenly took ill, left the service, and on getting home died." She had no doubt in her mind that the attack of the chief Imam had backfired on him.

CHAPTER FIVE

MISSIONARY JOURNEY TO THE UNITED STATES

As they ministered to the Lord and fasted, the Holy Spirit said, "Now separate to Me Barnabas and Saul for the work to which I have called them." [3] *Then, having fasted and prayed, and laid hands on them, they sent them away. Acts 13:2-3.*

In a dream in 1997, the Lord told me to go to the United States of America to start a church. I was hesitant because I didn't know how to start a church, and I did not want to leave my family without providing for their upkeep. Our sachet water business was barely able to sustain us because there were many unlicensed producers. NAFDAC, the regulating body, was also corrupt. Despite the approval of our product, they constantly caused trouble in order to pressure us to offer bribes, which we never did. The police also obstructed business by stopping our delivery truck frequently, expecting a bribe, which we never gave. These challenges did not encourage me to answer the call.

While still dragging my feet, I had a dream that I would be invited to manage a new bank. When I told my pastor, he told me to take the job if it came. A few months after my dream, I received an invitation to interview for the position of Managing Director of a new bank. The bank already had Four Hundred Million cash reserve. Thinking that my dream had come true, I considered taking the job and working for three years to save money for my family's upkeep before leaving for the United States for missionary work.

About that time, a young evangelist who visited us often and always called me "Man of God," came to our house. As we talked, he asked, "Man of God, what are you doing now?" I was puzzled, not knowing how to respond. I told him about the call to the United States and also about the job I was expecting with the new bank. Suddenly, his countenance changed, and rebuking me, he said, "If you take that job, you will be grounded. Don't you know that the job is not from God? God told you to go to the United States and start a church. People are waiting for you there, and you want to take a job. If you take that job, you will be grounded." I was getting angry, thinking how dare he come to my house to talk to me like that, but I remained calm. As if she heard our discussion, after the young evangelist left, my wife told me, "I know that the Lord has called you. If you do not go, we will be suffering together here!" This finally persuaded me to prepare for the trip.

Miracle In London
With the consent of my wife, I left for the United States via London in January 1998. To avoid the long flight of fourteen hours to the United States, I always flew six hours to London, stayed for a week, and then left for the US. This was why I flew to London. I also intended to tell my friends in London about my conversion experience and my missionary journey to the US. My wife and I usually stayed with Richard, a family friend, whenever we went on vacation to London. On arrival, I told Richard about my conversion and urged him to accept Jesus Christ as his Savior and Lord. He was very surprised but did not comment. That night, he had an encounter with the Lord, who confirmed what I told him. In the morning, he told me about his encounter, and he accepted Jesus Christ as his Savior.

One night, his pregnant wife had excruciating pain and could not sleep. I thought that she was in labor. Perplexed, I asked that we pray, and as soon as we did, she fell asleep. In the morning, she went to the hospital and came back with a wonderful report. The pain she had in the night was from a fibroid in her womb. I didn't know that at the time we prayed. On examination, the doctor told her that the big fibroid had shrunk to thumb size. He inquired about what she did to

33

cause the fibroid to shrink. She told him what happened in the night. We rejoiced about what the Lord did. My friend and his wife were significantly impacted by the miracle, and their faith in Jesus Christ was established.

Establishment of the Church
I arrived in the United States in January 1998 with no idea of how to start a church. Getting to the house from the airport, I simply put down my luggage and said, "Lord, You told me to come to the United States to start a church. I obtained a U.S. visa, I bought my ticket, I got on the plane to come to the United States, and now I am here. I have done what I could do. I don't know how to start the church. If the church is to start, it has to be from You." I came to Ben Yinusa, my friend, whom the Lord had shown me in the vision for the work. I knew that he would have something to do with the establishment of the church. I told him my mission, and he told me of a church that started in his apartment but had just packed up because of the attitude of the General Overseer. While not discouraging me, he explained the challenges he would face in inviting people again to start another church.

Ben and two other men held a prayer meeting every Sunday evening. The first Sunday evening after my arrival, He took me to the prayer meeting. He introduced me to the man leading the prayers. I knew the man from my previous visits to the United States. I immediately told him that my mission in the United States was to establish a church. Ben was not a member of any church, but every Sunday morning, he would choose a church where we would worship. He always introduced me to the pastors of the churches, and I always let them know that I came to the United States to start a church. When Ben asked me why I shared my mission with the pastors, I told him that it was because I didn't want them to have a wrong impression. Some of the pastors invited me to minister at the time, and I honored their invitation.

The second time we attended the prayer meeting, the leader said that the Lord asked him to hand over to me to lead the prayers. I began leading the prayers, and a few weeks later, two women joined us. A little later, another woman joined us. The seven of us continued in prayer every Sunday evening. In my private prayers, I continued to ask the Lord to show me how to start the church. One day, the Lord told me that the people in the Sunday evening prayer meeting would move for the church to start, and I told Ben. The Sunday evening prayers continued until one evening when one of the three women interrupted it and, looking at the men, said, "What are we doing here? Why are you people not recording these messages? Have you heard what this man was saying before? How can people join us in this place? Is this how the church will start? Why can't we look for a place where we can use for a church?" Witnessing what I had related to him come to pass, Ben was stunned, and his disposition changed.

That Sunday evening, I was mandated to look for a place of worship for the church, and the following morning, I went in search. After a long search, I came to a building on Elmwood Avenue that I had always liked and wished was our church. The little sign on the building that I had not noticed before read Spirit and Life Church. Excited, I took down the telephone number and called. The pastor picked up and told me they were looking for a church to share the maintenance expenses of the building with. He gave me an appointment to walk through the building. Before the date, in Revelation 3:8, the Lord ministered to me that He had given me an open door. I decided to invite one of the women to the appointment. To confirm the word of the Lord, the pastor opened every door in the building, even those that I considered unnecessary. We agreed to use the premises from 1pm to 3pm for our Sunday service after they finished their service at 12.30pm. Our church started with three members and me as the pastor. A family joined us for the first service

35

to give us support. The Lord began His amazing works, and
the church began to grow.

Boston Branch

I met a man at Grace Bible Church in Swansea, MA, who
had a hairdressing salon on Blue Hill Avenue in Boston, MA.
I visited him often whenever I went to the area. He asked
that I bring him tapes of our sermons so that he could give
them to some of his clients. I took tapes to him regularly, and
he gave them out. Those who got the tapes told him that they
would like to attend our church but that it was too far. He
said that if I came to minister to them, he would let me use
his salon on Sundays. I was excited, and the Boston church
started in the year 2000. On Sundays, we held services from
10am to 12 noon in Boston and in Providence from 1pm to
3pm. We also had Holy Ghost Power Service in Providence
on Sundays from 10pm to 12 midnight. The Lord did
wonders in healing, deliverance, and blessings.

Boston Sermon

One time, I started studying from Monday to prepare my
sermon for the Boston service, and I did not receive anything
from the Lord. So, on Saturday evening, in desperation, I
told the Lord, "Lord, I have been studying since Monday to
prepare the sermon for Boston. Today is Saturday, and I
have nothing for them." Then the Lord said, "You did not
ask me." I asked the Lord to forgive me and then asked Him
what He wanted me to tell the church. He said, "Go to John
chapter 5." As soon as I opened to John chapter 5, the
Scriptures lit up. I was filled with excitement. I was fed and
ready to pour out. That Sunday, as I began to preach, there
was a hunger and stirring in the people. Many could not sit
still. Noticing that, I told them how the Lord gave me the
word the previous night. I knew I needed to stop them from
thinking that it was my own knowledge or effort that
produced the sermon. Through that experience, I learned that
I could not rely on my effort to prepare a sermon for the

36

people of God. From that time, I always preferred the Holy Spirit to tell me what He wants me to say to His people, and that has eliminated any kind of pressure.

The Entire Church Baptized In The Holy Spirit

I was led to prepare a three-part teaching on the Baptism of the Holy Spirit. I was teaching the first part in Boston, and not more than twenty minutes into the teaching, the Lord said, "I am ready to baptize them now." In my mind, I felt that the people needed to get the basics before the baptism. So I continued teaching, and the Lord said again, "I am ready to baptize them now." So I packed my notes and told the people what the Lord said. We started praising the Lord, and suddenly everyone was baptized in the Holy Spirit, speaking in tongues. It was a dramatic, powerful, and amazing day. We practically experienced Acts 10:44-46.

Fetus Heartbeat Restored

A lady contacted me about her pregnant friend because the doctors said that the fetus in her womb had no heartbeat and needed to be evacuated. I was taken aback because I did not know what to do. Then the Lord told me that if I put my hand on my ear and heard heartbeats, the fetus still had a heartbeat. This sounded strange to me because I didn't understand what putting my hand on my ear had to do with the fetus that had no heartbeat. Somehow, I decided to do what the Lord said. So I put my right hand on my right ear, and I heard a rhythmic sound like a heartbeat. I was encouraged to pray for the pregnant woman, assuring her that the heartbeat of the fetus would be restored. I told her that when she got to the hospital, she should ask for another ultrasound before the procedure. When the ultrasound was done, it was discovered that the fetus still had a heartbeat and was not evacuated.

37

Stiff Neck Of Three Years Healed

Whenever I finish preaching at the Holy Ghost Power Night in our church, I minister to the people. In one of the services, a woman who had a scarf around her neck asked me to pray for her, saying that she had a stiff neck. As I reached out my hand to touch her neck and pray, she shouted, " I am healed. I am healed!" She began to move her neck in all directions to show that she had been healed. I looked at her incredulously, thinking that she was faking. Realizing that I did not believe her, she said, "Pastor, I am a nurse by profession. My neck had been stiff for three years. I traveled to Nigeria, and while driving with children in the car, in traffic, a person visible only to me struck me with an axe. Since then my neck had been stiff but now I am healed." This miracle from the Lord still amazes me.

A Woman With 18 Year Old Daughter Gave Birth Again

Someone introduced a woman to me for prayers. The woman said that after the birth of her daughter, who was 18 years old, she could not conceive again. She said that her husband started dating another woman who was now pregnant by him. Though sorrowful and fearing that she had lost her husband because of her condition, I assured her that the Lord would change her story. I prayed with her and counseled her not to fight the woman, her husband's mistress. A few months later, the husband's mistress gave birth. She came to me weeping. I comforted her and was inspired to tell her to buy baby clothes for the child of the mistress. It was not an easy thing for her to accept, but by the grace of God, she did so. A few months later, she became pregnant and was overjoyed. Her husband returned to her. By the time her daughter turned 19, she gave birth. Her husband bought her a Jeep, and their family was made whole. Glory be to God!

Reward Of Obedience For A Barren Woman

A woman who did not attend our church came to one of our midweek services. Standing before me and without asking anything, I was led by the Holy Spirit to tell her that she should continue doing good. She broke down sobbing and said that before leaving her house, she had just decided not to help the relatives of her husband anymore because they did not appreciate her generosity. She promised to obey the voice of the Lord. Somehow, I knew she desired to have a child, and I prayed for her. About seven months later, I saw the woman, and she was heavy with child.

Miraculous Purchase of a House
A lady in the church said that she would like to buy a house, and I prayed with her. She had no credit record at all. When she spoke to a bank, they asked her to produce her utility bills, and she did. She got approved and then bought a house. She then told her friends that it was not difficult to buy a house and that all they needed were their utility bills. She took a number of them to the same bank, and they were all rejected for lack of credit. This was when she realized that her house was a miracle from God.

Miraculous Restoration of a Minister
A member of our church told me one day to accompany him to speak to a lady. According to him, the lady had been a pastor for many years but had stopped attending church. On the way, I asked the Lord, "What can I say to your servant? She has been a pastor before me. What can I possibly tell her?" Then the Lord told me to tell her that she was like the prodigal son and that she was the one who left Him and that He never left her. After getting to the house and exchanging pleasantries, we got to the reason I came to see her. I told her only what the Lord said and no more. I did not add to or take away from it. To my amazement, the lady broke down and wept. After some time, she was composed. She was in church the following Sunday.

One Sunday, I asked her to join the choir. She was taken aback because she had not practiced with them. She served in the choir from that day. She was consistent and devoted herself to the work of the Lord. About two years later, we appointed her as the pastor of our Boston branch.

Try Jesus For 6 Months And See What Happens
I knew a young man living a carefree and ungodly life. Over time, he grew close to me, and that gave me the opportunity to minister to him. One day, I told him, "Your lifestyle is not a profitable one. Jesus Christ is who you need. If you give your life to Jesus Christ and nothing changes in six months, then go back to your lifestyle." Then he asked, "Did you say six months?" I said, "Yes, but in those six months, make sure you are fully committed to Him." Then he said six months is a short time and that he would do what I said. A month after he committed to the Lord, he came to me weeping and told me of his regret. Not understanding what he meant, I asked him how he could have regrets, and then he said that his regret was that he did not commit to the Lord sooner. He then told me of the wonders the Lord did in his life that month. He grew fervent in the Lord and now pastors a church in Texas.

The Healing Word
In the year 2001, I had a visit from two pastors who informed me of the death of Owolabi Owoyemi, my younger brother. I was heartbroken. My mother had only two of us. I had been in the US for three years and was only able to visit Nigeria once. That I was not available to console his children broke my heart. I wept continuously because I felt alone. The pastors, being unable to console me, left after doing the best they could. I wept profusely after they left. I felt paralyzed, unable to do anything. Loneliness overshadowed me, and I said in my heart, "Now I am alone." Immediately, the Lord spoke to me, saying, "Why do you say that you are alone? You are not alone. I am with you." Those words were miracle words because as soon as the Lord spoke them, my sorrow disappeared. The sense of loss vanished. Nothing in

40

me reflected the loss of my brother. Peace came. I was healed and filled with joy. The Lord gave me the oil of joy for mourning. Three days later, I ministered at a revival service of the Nigerian Council of Ministers. Seeing my joy, people asked, "Didn't they say that he just lost his younger brother?" The joy of the Lord blotted out my sorrow.

The Garment of Praise

I ministered at a church in Warwick, Rhode Island. After the preaching, I decided to pray with the people. While praying, I heard a woman wailing at the back of the church. The sound was so sorrowful it could not be ignored. I went to her. Her husband was standing by her, trying to console her. I asked her what was wrong, and she replied that she was depressed. I was perplexed, and not knowing what else I could say, I laid my hand on her and prayed. I was surprised that as soon as I started praying, the woman was baptized in the Holy Spirit. She spoke in tongues and started laughing. Her countenance changed. She was radiant and filled with joy. Her depression vanished, and we glorified God.

Pastor's Son Saved

The pastor's wife told me that she wanted her son saved but had prayed without results. I shared the testimony of my mother's salvation with her and assured her that her son would be saved. We used the same Scripture in Isaiah 60:21 and also Acts 16:31 to pray. A few months later, the woman saw me and, beaming with smiles, said, "Pastor Femi, my son is saved. Both he and his friend were saved at the same time." Hallelujah!

Poverty To Prosperity

At the inception of the church, I noticed that our parking lot looked like a junkyard. The cars were dilapidated, rusted, and one of them, in particular, was bent. It moved diagonally, like a crab. I was so disturbed that I pleaded with the Lord, saying, "Father, these are your children. Bless them and

41

remove from us the shame of a car park that looked like a junkyard." Most of the members were on a minimum wage of $6 an hour, working at group homes as Certified Nursing Assistants - CNA - at the time. Thinking of how to improve their condition, I went to the Department of Health in Providence with one question in mind. I met the officials and asked, "What can a CNA do to improve earnings?" They told me that they could study for one year to become an LPN - Licensed Practical Nurse. I asked them how much a LPN would earn and was told that the going rate was $18 an hour! I asked again, "What can one do after LPN and they told me that LPN can study to become Registered Nurse. They also said that a Registered Nurse can study to become a Doctor. I was stunned but relieved at the same time because I knew that there is a way out of poverty for the people.

I began to teach that members should go back to school. Many told me that it would be difficult because of their bills and I simply told them that if they go back for LPN, they would earn their current annual income in four months. This motivated many to return to school. Many became LPN and others RN. Some even earned their doctorate degree in nursing. Within a few years, some of them relocated to other states to head nursing departments of hospitals! The people of God prospered, bought homes, new cars, and the state of our parking lot changed. The Lord touched His people to accept good counsel and thereby took away our reproach.

It is important to teach the people of God how to improve their living conditions and support them in doing so. Acting on the word of God is more practical than night vigils.

Failure In Real Estate Licensing Examination Ended
One of our elders asked his friend to see me. He studied hard for his Real Estate License but never passed the exams. That prevented him from practising as a Real Estate Agent and severely limited his earnings capacity. When he met with me,

I prayed with him and assured him that the Lord would help him. He sat for the next exams and passed. The Lord helped him, and because of the miracle he received from the Lord, he became a member of our church.

Frustration In Passing Pharmacy Exams Terminated
One of the two people at the Sunday prayer meetings that gave birth to the church was a member of another church. He was in the same church as his brother-in-law, who could not pass his pharmacy exams. He had failed so many times, lost confidence, and could not practice as a pharmacist. The man came to join our church, saying that his brother-in-law told him that if he wanted to pass his pharmacy exams, he should join our church. I encouraged him with words of faith to build up his trust and confidence in God. I constantly assured him that the Lord would help him pass his next exams. We prayed, and by the grace of God, he passed.

Though he saw the grace of God, he was still apprehensive about passing the board exams required for certification to practice as a pharmacist in the state. I encouraged him in the Lord again, and we prayed, asking the Lord to finish the work that He began and to glorify Himself. To the glory of God, he attempted the board exams only once and passed. His frustration was alleviated, and the embargo on his profession and progress was lifted. Glory be to God.

CHAPTER SIX

RETURN TO NIGERIA

From there they sailed to Antioch, where they had been
commended to the grace of God for the work
which they had completed.
Acts 14:26

In January 2002, I knew that I had to return to Nigeria. I sent for the General Overseer of the church, and he came to the US. We had a handing-over service, and I handed over the two churches in Boston, MA, and Providence, RI, to him. A few days later, the General Overseer asked me if I was taking any vehicle back to Nigeria. Since I had none to take, I told him so. My focus was on my reunion with my family, whom I had not seen for three years. I told him that I believed that I would have a car to use when I got to Nigeria.

A few months earlier, I had prayed with a person who sued a company for damages and asked the Lord to resolve the matter in his favor. The company began to manipulate the system against him, and not being sure of a just outcome, he came to me again. I assured him that the matter would be resolved in his favor, and without thinking, I heard myself saying, *"When a snake is cut in two and is still going forward, it will eventually die."* A few days after my dialogue with the General Overseer, the person came and told me that the case was resolved in his favor. Then he said that he had promised in his heart that if he won the case, he would give me twenty percent of the settlement money. He then gave me a check for eleven thousand dollars, and with the money, I bought two vehicles, which I took to Nigeria!

Jesus Christ asked the disciples, *"When I sent you without money bag, knapsack, and sandals, did you lack anything?" So they said, "Nothing." Luke 22:35.* Just as the disciples had their needs met even when they had no money,

44

I also had my needs met. This miracle taught me that we will lack nothing in the service of the Lord. The fact that we do not have what we need right now does not mean that the Lord will not provide. He is absolutely dependable.

God Comforted a Family Friend.
I arrived in Nigeria in January 2002 and after some months, I decided to visit one of my high school classmates and his wife. The wife was not home when I got there, and after exchanging pleasantries, I told him that I would return the following Saturday to see his wife. Three days later, I received a call that my friend's wife had passed away. I could not believe it. I decided to go to my friend's house and find out for myself. Upon getting there, I found it to be true. It was devastating, and my friend was distraught. While weeping, he said, *"Femi, you are a pastor. Tell me, how can this happen? My wife was not sick. I was about to talk to the vigilante in the early morning when she asked me to sit down, lay down on my lap, and then she was gone. We just moved to this house three months ago. She spent more money on building this house. How can I be in this house when she is gone? I don't think I can go on without my wife. Tell me, how can this happen?"* My friend and his wife were very close. They played with each other like kids whenever they visited us and when we visited them. They enjoyed each other's company so much.

I was speechless and didn't know what to tell him. I had no words to comfort him. I only told him of my experience with the passing of my younger brother and prayed, asking the Lord to speak to him. After the prayer, I assured him that the Lord Himself would speak to him. Many of our classmates came to be with him, and after a while, we left. The following day, I went to see him again. Immediately he saw me, he laid hold of my hand and took me to his bedroom and said, *"You were right. The Lord spoke to me from Job 14. Now I understand. I am comforted. Thank you so much."*

45

Though still feeling sad about the sudden loss of his wife, I was relieved and grateful that the Lord consoled him.

The Lord Paid My Loan
The bank overdraft that I took in 1993 to buy the house increased to two million Naira, and I had no means of repaying it. Wanting to release our residential house, which was the collateral, I tried to sell the house, but we had no buyer. I contacted the bank to negotiate the release of the collateral in exchange for the house that I bought. While trying to do this, the Federal Government of Nigeria set up a Bad Debt Recovery Tribunal to help recover debts from defaulters. The tribunal was empowered to put defaulters in jail until they paid up. I received a summons to the tribunal. We could only afford to hire a fresh law school graduate, but the bank retained a SAN (Senior Advocate of Nigeria).

I asked the bank's lawyer to take the house I purchased and release our residential house, which I used as collateral. He sent his assistant to inspect the property. Upon inspection, he assured me that he would recommend the acceptance of my offer. I brought him back home to entertain him, and upon seeing our house, he changed his mind. I felt then that it was a mistake to bring him to our house. With no funds to redeem the loan, the case continued at the tribunal.

Everywhere I went to minister, someone would tell me that the Lord said my ministry was not in Nigeria but in the United States. I was not willing to listen because I had made up my mind not to return to the United States when I left in January 2002. For the four years that I was in the United States, I was not with my family. I did not want my family and I to experience that again. The Lord continued to send people to tell me to return to the United States. I still had no means of paying the debt. I had to appear before the Bad Debt Recovery Tribunal, and I was reluctant to leave my wife holding the bag. Again, the Lord sent a very close

46

pastor friend to tell me that my ministry was not in Nigeria but in the United States. Finally, the Lord told me to return to the United States, saying, *"Your file is no longer in the bank. I have paid the bank."* I was puzzled because, as a former banker, that was difficult to understand. However, I accepted the word of the Lord and returned to the U.S., but I was filled with anxiety, not knowing how the case would be resolved.

My wife continued to appear before the tribunal with our lawyer, but our lawyer never got called to offer a defense. My wife told me that whenever the case was called, the SAN would utter nonsensical statements, and the judge would adjourn the case. This happened several times. The last time the case was called, the SAN was incoherent again, and the judge adjourned the case, but this time beyond the tenor of the tribunal. When the court clerk reminded the judge that the tribunal would cease to function before the date of adjournment, the judge insisted that she would not hear the case before that date. The tribunal ended, and so did the bank's claim. I did not pay the overdraft, our residential house was not taken, and the house that I purchased remained in our possession.

My anxiety resolved nothing because God did everything. As Job 42:2 says, *"God can do everything."* He can take away your loan file from the bank. He can pay your loan. He can confuse the expert in order to give you a break. Our fresh law graduate lawyer did not say a word in the case except to introduce himself at the tribunal as our defense counsel. It is not by might nor by power. When God is in control, there is no need to worry. He can do all things. He is our advocate. Glory be to His holy name.

CHAPTER SEVEN

BACK TO THE UNITED STATES

Then after some days Paul said to Barnabas,
"Let us now go back and visit our brethren
in every city where we have preached the word of the Lord,
and see how they are doing."
Acts 15:36.

I returned to the United States in 2004, in obedience to the Lord's instruction. I did not return to Providence, Rhode Island, because of the less than amicable relationship among the ministers. In the four years that I was the pastor of the churches in Boston and Providence, there was never a time I settled any quarrel among the members. There was love and harmony among us. After my departure, the Boston branch collapsed due to neglect. Not wanting to be involved in the politics, I decided to go to Maryland. I joined Newness of Life Bible Church in Camp Springs. I had a very good relationship with the pastor of the church, Bishop James Mills, and his family. He was happy to have me in the church. The strife in Providence escalated, but I refused to get involved because I promised Bishop Mills that I was there to stay. I felt that it would be hypocritical to suggest going back to Providence.

Down Syndrome Cleared
A woman who was a member of the Providence church had one son, but her husband, not wanting another child, avoided intimacy with her. Being a young woman, she desired to have another child. She said that her husband did not inform her before their marriage that he wanted only one child. We asked the Lord to give her another baby. The woman said that after a long while, one night, the husband was intimate with her, and she conceived. With joy, I thanked the Lord for the miracle. I then began to prophesy about the child and I

asked her to write the prophecy. While in Maryland, I received a call from the woman, and she was weeping. After calming her down, she told me that the doctors said that the baby must be evacuated because of Down syndrome and that a date was already set for the surgery. I told her that the child could not have Down syndrome because of the prophecy I gave at her conception. I reminded her that God cannot lie, and I prayed with her. I gave her some Scriptures and asked her to confess them daily while laying hands on her belly. I also told her to ask her doctor for another evaluation on the day of the planned evacuation. Upon getting to the hospital, she asked for another evaluation, and the doctors were surprised to find no trace of Down syndrome in the child. The child was born perfect. She has turned out to be exactly as the Lord said by the prophecy given about her.

Return To Providence
In a dream one night, I found myself sitting in an elevated place near a road. I saw that a young boy crossing the road was crushed by a vehicle. The police investigating the accident came to me and said that I was under arrest. I was surprised and wondered why I should be arrested for something I was not involved with. As I pondered what the dream could mean, the Lord told me that if I didn't go back to Providence, He would hold me responsible for what happens there. The vision disturbed me but I was not willing to go. Stanley, an elder in the Maryland church called me a few weeks later and said, *"Pastor Femi, I used to hear the Lord very clearly in the past but because of my fault, I lost the gift, but it is now returning to me. The Lord told me that you must return to the church you started in Providence."* He then gave me the Scripture that the Lord gave him about the condition of the church.

I had another vision and saw that the church was being nursed by incompetent midwives and it was gradually dying. The Scripture that Elder Stanley gave was consistent with

49

that vision, and I knew that I had to return to Providence. I spoke to Bishop Mills, and he agreed that I should go. The strife among the leaders of the church had escalated by the time I returned. The General Overseer reached out to the Bishop of his former church, who called a meeting with the leaders of the church and asked me to attend. At the meeting, I wept much because I didn't want to return to the church, but I knew I had to obey the Lord. When I asked the Bishop why the Lord wanted me to return to the church, he said that it was because the Lord did not want the work that He used me to do in establishing the church to be destroyed. I summoned courage and faced the task. Reconciliation was not easy. The presiding pastor of the church left despite all my efforts to reason with him. The choir left with the pastor, and we had to start from scratch. It was very tough to restore the church. People's faith had been shaken, and fellowship was sluggish, but the Lord helped us.

Excruciating Pain Disappeared
One day, as I ministered in a church service, people drew my attention to something unfolding at the back of the church. A woman was in pain, weeping, and could not walk. I stopped the preaching and asked that she be helped to the front. She was brought to me. With both of us facing the church, I faced and asked what the problem was, and she said that she had excruciating pain in her leg. Then I said, *"I will not pray for you. You will deal with this yourself."* From the response of the congregation, I knew they did not approve of my declaration, but I was not concerned about their approval. I was determined to do what the Lord inspired me to do.

Quoting 1 John 4:4, I said, "The Bible says, 'You are of God, little children, and have overcome them, because He who is in you is greater than he who is in the world." Then I asked her, "Do you believe this?" She said, "Yes." I asked again, "Who is in you?" Still weeping, she said, "Jesus Christ." Then I asked, "Who is in the world?" She replied, "Satan."

50

Then I told her that she should command Satan to remove his hands from her leg. She did, but the pain did not leave. Then I said, "Do you want this pain in your leg?" She said, "No." I told her again, "I am not going to pray for you. You have to do this yourself." Then I told her that she did not sound convincing when she commanded Satan to remove his hands from her leg. I told her to command with authority, and when she did, the pain vanished. She ran around the church jubilantly. That day, I did not determine in advance what I was going to do. The Lord spontaneously used me to show to the church that they have authority over the works of darkness, and that if they believe the word of God and act on it, the Lord would back them up. Glory be to the Almighty.

Daughter's Wedding
When I returned briefly to Lagos in 1999, I sent our daughter, who had an accident on the motorbike at Ile-Ife, to England to further her education. She enrolled in King's College. After returning to the United States, the Lord told me that our daughter would not give us a long notice for her wedding. My income was still five hundred dollars a month. I knew that I could not save up for the wedding. So, I trusted the Lord to provide what we needed whenever the wedding would take place. As the Lord said, we had less than three months' notice for the wedding. Just before the wedding, the house that we had been trying to sell for many years was sold, and we had adequate provision for the wedding.

The Lord, who told me that our daughter would not give us a long notice for her wedding, ordered all things. Philip, a young man who usually assisted us in logistics, called me during the wedding reception and told me that the wedding was like a society wedding. The Lord beautified us. He gave glory to His name, and people wondered at the grace of God upon us.

Miracle College Admission

Before I returned to the United States, one of our sons gained admission to Covenant University. It was one of Nigeria's prestigious private Christian universities. The admission was a miracle. Our son insisted that he would not seek admission to any other university and did not apply to any. Though qualified, we had no money to buy the admission form. Admission closed, and we had no clue about what to do. Somehow, the university, for the first time since its inception, reopened the admission process, and by that time, we had money to buy the admission form. Our son applied and was offered a place, but we had no money for tuition. Many parents who came with money seeking admission for their children were denied. I returned to the United States without paying our son's tuition.

Miracle Provision For College Tuition Of Our Children

Shortly after my arrival in the United States, I was invited to minister in a few churches and received a total of about five hundred dollars in honorarium. The Lord told me to send the money for our son's tuition. I called and told my wife what the Lord said. She told me that the university informed her that our son would be allowed in class if we made a deposit that is the Naira equivalent of exactly five hundred dollars! So I sent the money, and our son was allowed in class, but we still had no money to pay the balance. Not long after, the house was sold, and after our daughter's wedding expenses, we had enough money left over for our son's tuition at Covenant University and the tuition of our younger daughter at the same university. Our eldest son's tuition up to master's degree level at Babcock University, another prestigious private university, was also funded.

The faithfulness of God is indisputable. I remember that it was the Lord who told me to give the proceeds of the shares that I sold to pay my children's school fees to the pastor. It was after I obeyed that He gave us the house. I paid only

Two Hundred Thousand Naira from my pocket. The balance was part of the overdraft of Two Million Naira, that the Lord paid for me. The Lord used the proceeds from the sale of the house to pay our daughter's wedding expenses and the tuition of three of our children in reputable private universities!

Who would have known that the Lord would do this? The Bible says, "Obedience is better than sacrifice." God rewards obedience. I now understand that He reserved the house and allowed its sale only at the right time. He received a deposit for my children's school fees through the proceeds of shares that He told me to give to the pastor. Through the sale of the house, He multiplied it and made it sufficient for the wedding of our daughter and the college tuition of our children. I did not have to work for them. The Lord paid it all. The timing of the Lord is perfect!

Visible Peace
In 2005, I went to a shoe store on Elmwood Avenue in Providence to see an elderly friend. The man was not at the store, but the owner was there. I decided to look at some of the shoes; perhaps I might find something that I liked. While still browsing, the owner of the store, as if screaming, began to say, "Where have you got this peace?" When I turned to face him, he continued, "Where have you got this peace? You have peace written all over you." He then began to relate a tale of woes about his life, family, relationships, and business. After calming him, I told him, "My peace comes from Jesus Christ. If you turn to Him, you will have the same peace." I then prayed with him and left. That day, I realized that the peace of the Lord is visible.

About three months later, I visited the man. He had another friend with him. As soon as I entered, he pointed at me and told his friend, "This is the man that I am talking about." He then told me that since we prayed, his life has turned around.

He said that he has peace in his family and relationships. While he was talking to me, many people came to buy shoes. He said that after our prayer, instead of struggling for money to buy shoes like before, a company contracted to give him shoes on credit and receive payment from him after he sold them. In addition, he said that his sales skyrocketed. Pointing to the buyers, he said, "Look at them. Who goes to a store to buy three, four, or five pairs of shoes? But this is what they are doing here." I looked, and saw that he was right; only a few of the buyers bought two pairs. Others bought more.

Visible Peace Confirmed

Over the years, I have shared the testimony of the visible peace of God with the church. In 2024, some ministers came to hold a three-day seminar in our church. On the last day, one of them, talking to the church, pointed at me and said, "The peace of God is on this man. You can see it." The visible peace of God upon my life was confirmed to the church that day. This confirmed the word that the Lord spoke before my salvation when He said, "Give your life to Jesus, and you will have peace." God is faithful. He does what He says. He fulfilled His promise and gave me visible peace.

Business Is Ministry

I went to prepare my taxes with a man introduced to me by an elder of our church. After preparing my taxes, we talked, and he was fascinated with my testimony. We both had similar education - he being a CPA and MBA, and I being a CMA and MBA. He did not charge me for his service but asked that I pray for him and his wife. They held hands, and just as I was about to pray, the Lord told me to ask them if they would rather own their business or let it be a ministry where they would serve God. After asking, they said they would work for the Lord as ministers, and I prayed for them. Over the years, their business grew, the Lord enlarged them, and humbled those who worked against their interests. All the things that the Lord revealed whenever we prayed came to pass. They have become prominent in their field, and others envy them.

Spell Of Barrennes Broken
We had a woman in our church who had been married for many years without children. On a Sunday service, I asked her to come out for prayer, but she was shy. One elder encouraged her and brought her out for prayer. I prayed and made a declaration that she would be pregnant and bear children. Three months later, I saw people whispering, pointing to the woman, and marveling at the works of God. She was pregnant! She gave birth to a very beautiful girl. After we departed from the church in 2008, I met her in the parking lot of a store one day. She was carrying a child and busy instructing the two toddlers in front of her. Seeing this, I laughed. She also laughed. I reminded her that she had been very reluctant to come to the front of the church that Sunday. She said that she was petrified, and I said, "Now you are busy because the Lord has blessed you with many children." Acknowledging what the Lord did, we laughed heartily, marveled, and praised God for His great and wonderful work.

The word of God is true. Deuteronomy 7:14 says, *"You shall be blessed above all peoples; there shall not be a male or female barren among you or among your livestock."* Exodus 23:26 says, *"No one shall suffer miscarriage or be barren in your land; I will fulfill the number of your days."* God needs people to fulfill His purpose. Strictly speaking, based on the choice of God, He cannot fulfill His purpose on earth without people. In fact, it is for this reason that He instituted marriage, because Malachi 2:15 says, *"But did He not make them one, having a remnant of the Spirit? And why one? He seeks godly offspring…"* God brings a male and a female together in marriage, makes them one, so that they can bring up godly offspring to serve God. When Hannah vowed that if God would give her a son, she would give him to serve the Lord, God did not hesitate to answer her request. After she gave the son to God, she received five more children from the Lord!

Do you want to serve God in your marriage? Do you want to raise godly offspring for God? If you won't take possession of them as your personal property but want to be a steward of God, to have children that you will train to serve the Lord, nothing can keep you barren. He who gave a son to Sarah (Isaac), He who gave Hannah a son (Samuel), He who gave Samson to his mother, He who gave Elizabeth a son (John the Baptist), will give you children if you will train them to serve God. He still needs workers in His vineyard. Enlist yourself in the childbearing and childraising ministry today.

A Black Man Became President Of The United States
On 1st June, 1996, the Lord showed me a vision that a Black man became the president of the United States. In the vision, I saw that the man gave a great speech. I recorded the vision in my notebook. When, at the Democratic Convention of 2004, I saw Barrack Obama give a speech in Boston, Massachusetts, I was puzzled because, though I recognized him by the speech as the person referred to in my vision of 1996, he was not running for president. When he announced his run for president of the United States in February 2007, I began to tell people that Obama would become the next president of the United States. I preached a sermon titled, "A United States President in Prophecy." Most people did not believe that Obama could win the nomination of the Democratic Party, let alone the presidency. Many who were concerned for me cautioned that I was ruining my ministry by giving a false prophecy. I told them that it was not my word but the word of the Lord. I encouraged the people to believe that the Lord is able to make them whatever He wants them to be and put them in any position He desires for them. When Obama won the nomination, some began to lessen their criticism of me. When he won the election for

56

President of the United States, people acknowledged the integrity of the word of the Lord.

Failure To Pass Exams Terminated

A Cameroonian couple had three children and were having marital problems. They were on the brink of separation. In a counseling session, it became obvious to me that the source of their trouble was the financial pressure they faced due to the husband's incessant failure to pass his final medical exams. This made it impossible for him to work as a doctor. I prayed and asked the Lord to help him overcome that frustrating stagnation. They joined the church, and the Lord worked His wonders again. The man passed the next exams he took. The Lord gave them a breakthrough shortly after, and he secured a job as a doctor out of state. They relocated with joy to start a new life.

I pray that the Lord who helped this man will also break down all agencies of stagnation in your life, in the name of Jesus Christ. He will destroy all satanic tools set against your family in the name of Jesus Christ. Whatever the enemy is using to frustrate your progress, the Almighty God will neutralize it in the name of Jesus Christ. The grace of God upon your life will speak, and you will not be caged in the name of Jesus Christ. It is your turn to flourish in the name of Jesus Christ.

Multiple Miracles for a Realtor

During a visit to Nigeria, a man based in the United States spoke to his brother-in-law about his business problems. The brother-in-law, who was my junior in high school and a member of our church in Lagos, told the man to contact me on his return to the US. He made an appointment to meet with me after returning to the US. We met at the church, and he told me of his difficulties. The man came to the United States at eighteen, graduated as a pharmacist, and worked for many years before going into the real estate business, but at

57

age fifty, he was on the verge of losing everything. He had properties in Providence and Ohio. The 2008 real estate collapse severely affected his business. His properties in Providence were in foreclosure, and the bank filed a lawsuit against him. They threatened to seize his properties in Ohio to liquidate his loan. He flew from Ohio to Providence every week to negotiate with the bank, but without a breakthrough. In addition, he owed the IRS one hundred and fifty thousand dollars in back taxes. He planned to sell his apartment complex in Ohio, which he believed would fetch him a net income of fifty thousand dollars, and relocate to Nigeria.

1. Desolation Overturned

I told the man that it would be a disaster for him to run away with fifty thousand dollars after so many years of laboring in the United States. I assured him that the Lord would help him if we prayed. I also told him that I would be available to guide him as the Lord led me. He was persuaded, and after we prayed, I told him to ask the bank to appoint a Receiver Manager for the properties in Providence. I explained the role of a Receiver Manager to him and that this would free him from his weekly commute and give him time to look after the properties in Ohio.

The bank accepted his request, appointed a Receiver Manager, and he was relieved. We kept praying, and in the course of time, I visited him in Ohio, and we went to his properties and prayed. On one of those visits, I noticed that he was worried, and when I inquired, he told me of a letter he received from his lawyer telling him that the case about the Providence properties was coming up. To represent him, the lawyer asked for twelve thousand dollars, but he did not have the money. I told him to send the lawyer an email telling him that he had no money and would not need his services, and that if he went to court, he would be doing so without any charge. He was even more worried, but I persuaded him to write the email, and he did. The following

58

day, the lawyer called him after court to tell him of the miracle that the Lord did. According to the lawyer, everyone who bid for the properties bid less than the amount he owed the bank, but at the last minute, an unknown person entered and bid the exact amount that he owed. The judge ruled the property sold, and the man paid. The case was resolved without any recourse to him. He paid neither the bank nor the lawyer anything.

2. IRS Back Taxes Resolved.
After this, his accountant received a letter from the IRS saying that the amount he owed could be paid in installments at his discretion without penalty. The accountant said that he had never seen any such decision from the IRS since he had been in practice. I had to persuade him several times to make the first payment to the IRS as an acceptance of the offer.

3. Tenant's Lawsuit Dismissed
While this was happening, the daughter of one of the tenants in his apartment complex filed a lawsuit claiming two hundred thousand dollars in damages for discrimination. We prayed, asking the Lord to dismiss the lawsuit. Not long after, he returned to the complex after running an errand one afternoon to find police officers around the building. He approached one of them, introduced himself, and inquired why the police had come to the building. The man who said he was the Chief of Police told him that one of his tenants had gone missing. It was the man whose daughter had filed the lawsuit. He then told the Chief of Police that the daughter of the man had a lawsuit filed against him for two hundred thousand dollars, alleging discrimination. The Chief of Police, who knew the man and his daughter very well, said that he would go to court and give a deposition in his favor. He went to court as he promised, gave the deposition, and the case was dismissed.

4. New Insight Into Commercial Real Estate Business

On one occasion while we prayed, I received a word from the Lord for him. The Lord said that he did not know much about commercial real estate financing yet and that He would teach him. A few months later, he received an invitation to attend a conference on commercial real estate financing. He attended the conference, and when he returned, he called me, saying that the word of the Lord was true and that he had been financing his business in the wrong way. He said that, with the new insight he had gained, he would be able to acquire properties without any down payment. Later, he acquired more properties without a down payment.

5. Building Value Skyrocketed

About two years later, he told me that the apartment complex he wanted to sell for a profit of Fifty Thousand Dollars, and relocate to Nigeria was valued at Six Million Dollars!

If you allow fear in your heart, the enemy will deprive you of your inheritance. The man's fear would have destroyed his fortunes. He could have sold his properties worth millions of dollars for a profit of only Fifty Thousand Dollars! By encouraging him to trust the Lord, giving him good counsel, and praying, his business problems were resolved. Jeremiah 33:3 says, *"Call to me and I will answer you and show you great and mighty things you do not know."* God did not ignore any of our pleas. He resolved all the challenges. If by faith we wait on the Lord, He will give us relief from our troubles. Not only that, He will also increase us just as He showed the man a new technique for structuring commercial real estate deals that increased his portfolio.

The Lord will thwart all the schemes of the enemy to plunder you in the mighty name of Jesus Christ.

Expensive Suits For Almost Free

I told the Lord one day, "Father, *I need some dark suits.*" A few months later, I was walking around and praying at the church when I heard the Lord say, *"Go to the mall."* I went to my favorite store at the mall. While walking around, I kept saying in my mind, *"Lord, you asked me to come to the mall. I am in the mall. What do you want me to do in the mall?"* Then, I saw the door to a side room open. A man emerged, pointed to me, and said, "Eh you, come." Pointing to myself, I responded, "Me?" and he said, "Yes." So, I walked toward him. He then showed me many high-quality 100% worsted wool dark suits. I looked at their price tags and found they were expensive. As I turned to walk away, he said, "I will give them to you for ninety dollars each, and if you buy it, I will give you a ten-dollar rebate." That meant that each suit would be eighty dollars. So, I asked him, "What is wrong with them?" And he said, "Nothing." So I bought some of the suits. I realized that the Lord brought me to the store for the suits. Then I remembered that I had asked the Lord for dark suits many months earlier.

CHAPTER EIGHT

NEW MINISTRY COMMENCED

So Jesus said to them again, "Peace to you!
As the Father has sent Me, I also send you."
John 20:21.

Kingdom Lighthouse Church began in May 2009, after I left Christ Miracle Vineyard Church (CMVC) on September 30, 2008. In a vision around March 2007, the Lord told me, "It is time to begin your ministry." I recorded it in my notes at the time. I also recorded visions of the events and attacks that the Lord showed would come against my ministry in the church. I completely forgot the visions. When attacks began on me and my ministry, I decided to review my notes to find out if the Lord had told me anything that I might have missed. As I reviewed my notes, I found that I had recorded the events and attacks occurring, including the exact phrases and words people were speaking months before! I also found where I had written the instruction of the Lord, saying, "It is time to begin your ministry." At that time, I realized that the attacks occurred because I had overstayed my time in the church. I then decided to inform the church of the Lord's desire for me to begin my ministry.

The attacks did not wane even after my announcement. At the beginning of September, the elders of the church called me to a meeting and asked me to tell them exactly when I would leave. I felt as if I was being pushed out. I was surprised because I had not even thought about a date. So I told them that I would get back to them. Leaving the meeting, I went toward the altar to pray. While attempting to kneel down, I said in my mind, "Father, you have heard your children. What do you want me to tell them?" Before my knee touched the ground, the Lord said, "September 30."

I felt the date might not be logistically feasible because of what needed to be done before I left. Administrative and operating protocols had to be properly handed over. A new pastor would need to be appointed in consultation with the General Overseer, who was based in Lagos, Nigeria. The program for a handing-over service needed to be drawn up, etc. So, I called Bishop Simmons, my spiritual mentor, and without telling him what the Lord said, I informed him of the request of the elders for me to give them a date when I would leave. To my shock, Bishop Simmons replied, "Not later than October 1." This was a day after September 30! The words of Bishop Simmons confirmed the word of the Lord to me, and I knew that I had to leave by September 30, 2008.

I went full speed ahead to ensure that all that needed to be done was done. A new pastor was chosen in consultation with the General Overseer. Administrative and operating procedures were properly handed over. The handing over program was drawn up with the consent of the leadership of the church. In the remaining weeks of September, I focused on teaching what the Lord gave me to prepare them for the transition and the future. The handing over was peacefully and smoothly done on Sunday, September 30.

The God of all Grace
We lived in a rented apartment, and our monthly rent of seven hundred dollars was paid by the church. When we left the church on September 30, the church refused to pay our rent for October. I had no money to pay the rent, which was due on the 5th of the month, and my landlady forgave our rent. The church paid me a monthly salary of one thousand dollars at the end of each month. It took several weeks to convince the church to pay me the salary for the month of September. We had no oil to heat our apartment. My wife and children who joined me in the United States just over a year earlier were not used to the cold. We turned on the oven all day, hoping the heat from the kitchen would radiate to the

63

house, but it never did. Every night, we slept on cold beds, shivering. We persevered, and the grace of God kept us. It was a very difficult and trying time.

Nobody from the church visited us. They avoided us even in public. It was strange. Only one Christian sister came to visit, and when she saw our living conditions, she broke down and wept before us. Before she left, she gave us a check for five hundred dollars, and that was like fifty thousand dollars to us.

Miracle Accomodation
I was out visiting a friend one day when I received a call from Classical High School that I should come to take our children out of the school. Getting to the school, I was informed that our children were not residents of Providence and were therefore not qualified to be in the Providence school system. I didn't know how to solve the problem because the only way our children could return to school was for us to get accommodation in Providence. To the glory of God, the first person I called told me that there was a three-bedroom apartment available for rent. It was gas heated! We signed a lease that day, and armed with the lease, we took our children back to Classical High School the following morning. The teachers were happy to have them back. They told us that they couldn't have done anything to prevent their withdrawal because they were instructed by the Schools Department to send them out of school. We thanked them, left, and glorified God for resolving the issue.

After we related our experience to a friend later, he said that without doubt, someone from the church must have reported our children to the Schools Department to cause us trouble. He said it was another attack, but I did not believe him until his words were later confirmed. Knowing that we lived in Pawtucket, the person who reported us must have believed that we lied to register our children at Classical High School. But their admission was a miracle because, on the day of registration, my wife thought we could persuade the officials to register them. On getting there, as I motioned to speak, the official raised her hand and would not let me speak a word, but simply said, "Give me your driver's license," and I did. Without asking any questions, she registered the children based on the address on my driver's license! At the time I applied for my license, since I was temporarily staying with an elder of the church, I used the church address. Months after obtaining the license, I got an apartment in Pawtucket. I didn't know our children would be registered based on the address on my driver's license. I also did not remember that my license had the Providence church address. If I had, I would not have thought of persuading the official to register our children. Their registration was a miracle because if the official had allowed me to speak, I would have ruined their chances. The Lord used the official to seal my mouth.

You are Like Noah in the Ark
To begin our ministry, I wanted to move far away from Providence to shield myself and my family from further attacks. So my wife and I drove to Florida in search of a place. We found a five-bedroom house with a huge kitchen, dining room, and living room that I thought was big enough to start a church. The house had a swimming pool, and it was rent-free! I told our host that we would start the church there. With excitement, we left the location and went back to the house of our host. As soon as I sat on the couch in the living room, I heard the Lord say, *"Is it a big house you want or a ministry?"* Stunned, I told our host that Florida was not the place for the ministry, relating what the Lord just told me. I then told my wife that we would leave in the morning. Surprised, our host concurred, and my wife went into the bedroom to pack.

We left Florida early and headed to Ohio. The realtor friend who had received several miracles from the Lord through our ministry had expressed a desire to support the planting of a

65

church there. We spent the night in West Virginia and drove to Akron, Ohio, the following day. Our host was happy to see us, and the following day, we went out looking for a place for the ministry. After visiting Johnstown, among many others, and finding nothing, we decided to go to Pittsburgh. Our host told us that he had a house in Pittsburgh that we could use. He called his friend to meet us at the house and give us the keys. We drove to Pittsburgh, and the friend met us at the house. He tried all the keys, and not one opened the door. He decided to break the door lock, but I told him not to because I did not have a witness that the place was right for us.

We left the house and drove to the house of a young woman who was a member of our church in Providence before she moved to Pittsburgh. We asked her to introduce us to a Realtor who could show us around the city. She called the woman who helped her get her house. The woman agreed to take us around. However, the woman took us to the worst and wildest neighborhoods in Pittsburgh. We had never seen such places in our lives. At one point, I asked the woman why she was showing us the kind of places she did, and she replied that she wanted us to see places where we would find people like us. I was shocked and angrily rebuked her. Then she decided to show us one house in a nice neighborhood, but it was not suitable for a ministry.

Returning to the house of our host that night, I said, "Lord, we have been to Florida. We were in Ohio. Now we are in Pittsburgh and haven't found a place. Where is the place for the ministry?" Then the Lord said, "You are like Noah in the ark. Where the ark rests is the place for the ministry." At that point, I realized that we had no choice but to return to Providence. Waking up the following morning, we embarked on our journey back to Providence. We had driven more than three thousand miles within one week attempting to go far

66

away from Providence, only to return! If I had simply asked the Lord from the beginning, we would have been spared.

The Lord Paid Our Rent
Coming back, we moved into the apartment we secured in Providence. Our landlady having allowed us to apply the deposit paid at the beginning of the lease to our last month's rent in Pawtucket, we were able to make the first month's rent for the new apartment. Our new landlord was Nigerian. The day we moved in, I told the Lord, "The landlord of this house is a Nigerian who is younger than I. I don't want to be embarrassed." I said this because I had no savings and no money to pay rent.

I left for Maryland a few days after we moved in. I called to greet Bishop Mills, and he asked that we meet for breakfast. At breakfast, Bishop Mills told me that he needed sixteen thousand dollars to meet church expenses. I said, "Bishop, you know that if I have the money, I would give it to you right away." While acknowledging that, he then shocked me by saying, "Pastor Femi, the Lord is speaking to me about you," and I said, "What is He saying?" Then he said, "The Lord said that I should pay your rent for the next six months" I was amazed. The Lord asked someone in need of money to pay my rent! Bishop Mills faithfully sent me the monthly rent for our apartment for those six months.

After the six months, we had a wonderful experience of the faithfulness and timeliness of God. Our rent was due on the 4th of the month, but one month I didn't have the money. It was a Saturday. I was in the house and didn't know what to do. Mid-morning, I got a call asking that I come to minister in Medford, MA, to a group of Indians. Our Indian ministry had started at the time. My wife and I left for Medford with no expectation because we neither asked for an offering nor was any collected for us whenever we ministered to them. That day, after I finished ministering, people began to give

67

us offerings. We received over nine hundred dollars. We got back home at about 9pm, and immediately, the landlord sent his son to ask for the rent. I was able to pay our rent. The Lord saw to it that I was not embarrassed.

Ministry Commenced
Shortly after we left the church, my wife located a church close to our apartment - Living Hope Assembly of God Church. We began worshiping with the church. The pastor of the church asked me to minister from time to time. When he asked us to join the church, I told him that since the Lord said that we should begin our ministry, joining the church would amount to disobedience. We continued the fellowship, and he allowed us to use part of the church for a weekly prayer meeting, and the Lord did wonders.

Prayers At The Plymouth Rock In Massachusetts
In October 2008, the Lord impressed upon my heart to go to Plymouth, MA, with my family and pray that the Lord would remember the covenant He had with the forefathers of the United States of America. I went to Plymouth, MA, with my family and prayed at the Plymouth Rock. Most people looked at us in a funny way as we prayed, but one or two joined us to pray. About three years later, I ministered at a Nigerian church that rented a church building in Stoughton, MA. The pastor of the church they rented, who was a woman, was at the service. As I ministered, I referred to the prayer at the Plymouth Rock. At the end of the service, the woman asked to see me. She asked me to confirm what she heard me say about the Plymouth Rock prayer. Having confirmed, she asked if I knew that there was a covenant made on the ship called the Mayflower Compact. I had never heard of it, and I told her so. She promised to mail a copy to me and also told me that it was available on the internet. She sent me a copy as she promised, and that increased my resolve to just believe what the Lord says. I never knew that there was a covenant signed by the pilgrims, but the Lord, who knew and

who was a party to the covenant, asked me and my family to pray. God never ignores His covenants.

67 Years Of Exhaustion Healed

At the end of one of the prayer meetings at Living Hope Assembly of God Church, a woman asked me to pray for her. When I asked what was the matter, she said, "I am always exhausted." Without touching her, I said, "You should not be exhausted. The word of God says, He gives power to the weak, and to those who have no might, He increases their strength. Receive your strength in the name of Jesus Christ." A few weeks later, the woman gave a testimony of her healing. She said that she was born with exhaustion and that the doctors thought she would not survive. She said that her marriage collapsed because of exhaustion. She said if she took a bath, she would have to lie down to regain her strength. She said that when people talked with her, she would be exhausted just listening to them. She then said, "Pastor, when you prayed for me, I felt nothing, but I am completely healed." I replied, saying, "When I prayed for you, I also felt nothing." The woman became the treasurer of our church. She ran errands for the church. She baked zucchini bread often for us, and whenever I asked her not to bother, she would say, "Pastor, what would I do with this energy other than to use it to serve God?" The sister was healed at 67 and served until she went to be with the Lord at 79 years.

Deliverance By The Holy Spirit

At another time at the prayer meeting, I told the people that the Holy Spirit would move among us as we praised the Lord. As we began to praise and worship, Pastor Cabral, the pastor of the church, who was in his office at the time, came out and laid prostrate on the floor, worshiping the Lord. One of the women had deliverance without anyone praying for her. It was a glorious day in the Lord.

69

Accident Victim Fully Restored

A man who attended our Bible study came one day, visibly shaken, and told me that his son, speeding on a motorbike at sixty miles an hour without a helmet, crashed and was rushed to the hospital. The doctor told him there was nothing they could do for his son and that he should not get his hopes up. I followed him to the hospital, and at the intensive care unit where his son was, we prayed. I declared that his son would recover and that there would be no trace of the accident in his life. Upon hearing that, the doctors told us to leave. The man then contacted his friend, who he said was a man of God that he respected, and his friend told him not to get his hopes up. He called and left a message on my phone about what his friend said, but I did not respond to him. Agitated, he came to accuse me that I didn't respond to his phone because I didn't care. Then I replied, "Do you want your son dead or alive? I went to the hospital with you and prayed that your son would live, but your friend, who did not go to pray for your son, told you not to get your hopes up and you want me to respond. I don't respond to such things." Realizing that he had wrongly accused me, he became calm.

Some time later, at our Friday Bible study, the man walked in with a tall, handsome young man. It was his son, fully recovered and without any side effects from the accident. The Lord made him perfectly whole. We rejoiced and glorified God for His marvelous works.

God Gave Me A Laptop

I needed to buy a laptop. At our Indian ministry meeting, I asked one of the computer engineers to recommend one with good specifications for me. After I got the specifications, I decided to go to Best Buy in South Attleboro to buy the laptop. On the way, the Lord told me not to buy it, so I returned home. After waiting a few weeks, I again left home for Bestbuy at South Attleboro to buy the laptop. I got as far as the premises of Cardis furniture in South Attleboro, then the Lord told me again not to buy the laptop. Again, I returned home. I didn't know why the Lord told me not to buy the laptop because I needed it. However, a few weeks later, I came home to find a package delivered to my house with my name on it. Thinking that it was a wrong delivery and that the delivery company would come back for it, I didn't open the package. About a week later, I received a call from Texas from someone who had lived with us, asking if I received the laptop that he sent to me. I told him about the package delivered to my house, and he confirmed that it was the laptop that he sent. When I opened the laptop, I was surprised that it was the exact specification that the computer engineer gave me.

These things amaze me and also teach me about the ways of God. His omniscience, omnipotence, mercy, and grace are clearly revealed. I also learned that the instructions of the Lord, if cherished and obeyed, always work for our good. I am learning to value the voice of the Lord that directs our daily lives. Indeed, a child of God who follows the voice of the Holy Spirit will be a mystery. The Lord Jesus Christ said in John 3:8 *"The wind blows where it wishes, and you hear the sound of it, but cannot tell where it comes from and where it goes. So is everyone who is born of the Spirit."* We should be like the wind, which no one can predict.

CHAPTER NINE

UPPER ROOM MINISTRY IN WARWICK

And they went out and preached everywhere,
the Lord working with them and confirming the word
through the accompanying signs.
Mark 16:20.

Rick Roderick and I approached the management of the Upper Room in Warwick to give us a place in their premises to minister to people on Sunday afternoons. They did, and we commenced the ministry. The Lord did many miracles, and here are a few of them.

A Smoker Was Delivered From Nicotine Addiction

After ministering one Sunday afternoon, I offered to pray with the people. I prayed for each person's request. I noticed that a woman sitting a few rows from me did not come forward for prayer. I pointed to her and asked her to come forward. When she got to me, a wave of nicotine hit me, and I almost choked. I knew she smoked and asked her, "You smoke?" She said, "Yes." I told her that the Lord is able to deliver her from the habit. Then she said, "Pastor, I have tried several times to quit, but I could not." I asked her if she really wanted to quit smoking, and she affirmed that she would like to. Then I told her to pray, saying, "Lord, I really want to quit smoking, and I have tried several times but could not. I do not have the power to quit. You are the only One who can help me. Take away the desire for cigarettes from me. In the name of Jesus Christ, deliver me from nicotine addiction." After she prayed as I instructed, I said, "Father, you have heard your daughter. Remove her desire for cigarettes, and deliver her from nicotine addiction." Six months later, I ran into the woman, and she said, "Pastor Femi, since the day you prayed for me, no cigarette has entered my mouth. Now, I am smoking for Jesus. Every

week, I gather people in my house for Bible study." Radiant
and very joyful, I was very happy to hear her testimony, and
we glorified God together.

Family Restoration
Another Sunday afternoon, a woman asked me to pray for
her. When I asked what she wanted to pray about, she said
that the relationship between her and her husband was not
good. After praying, the Lord laid on my heart to tell her not
to go to bed before her husband returned from work, but that
she should simply embrace him when he came home. She
came back to testify that when she embraced her husband on
his return home, he broke down and wept. That was the end
of the enmity and animosity in their marriage. Peace returned.

Marriage Of Upper Room Official
The day I saw one of the officials of the Upper Room, the
Lord made me prophesy that he would receive his bride. He
broke down and wept. I never knew that he was asking the
Lord for a wife. He showed me a woman some months later
that he wanted to marry. The Lord had me tell him that if he
married the woman, he would be miserable. He joined our
church, and the Lord gave him his longtime friend as a wife.
I officiated at their wedding.

Answered Prayer For The Upper Room President's Wife
Praying with the wife of the president of the Upper Room
one evening, the Lord ministered to me to tell her that her
long-awaited desire would soon be fulfilled, and I did. About
a year later, the woman, in a testimony, said that the Lord
granted her desire to adopt a son. She said that the Lord gave
her a son who fulfilled all that she desired.

Divine Support At The YMCA
We had numerous acts of divine support during our tenancy
at the YMCA. At a revival we held a few months into our
tenancy, an official of the YMCA alleged that one attendee

73

was rude to her. I was summoned before the YMCA Director, who told me of the incident. I contacted the official who lodged the complaint to deescalate the matter. She was willing to acquiesce, believing that the stress of her father's health at the time might have caused her to overreact, but the Director appeared unwilling. He threatened to terminate our tenancy agreement, unmindful of the disruption that would cause to the church. Refusing my plea, I walked out of his office, wondering why he was arrogantly opposing the work of the Lord by threatening to terminate our tenancy. The Director was fired that week.

We had no freedom with the Director. We often had seats taken from under us while in church service. Our services were interrupted many times to make room for yoga classes. However, when the yoga class was on, at a time we were supposed to use the space, we were made to wait until they finished. We were locked out of the premises many times and could only pray in the parking lot. The new Director worked with us. He gave us another space where we had no disruptions to our services. He provided us storage space for our equipment, and we didn't have to carry it in and out of the premises. This was a great relief. He also gave us the keys to the premises so that we could let ourselves in.

In the course of our tenancy, we noticed that many YMCA staff members who constrained or unnecessarily troubled us were fired. We didn't have to report them. It became clear that the Lord was fighting for us. The Lord blessed us, and we bought our own chairs. Chairs were no longer taken from under us, and we gave the YMCA permission to use our chairs whenever they needed to.

CHAPTER TEN

MINISTRY AMONG INDIANS

You have delivered me from the strivings of the people;
You have made me the head of the nations;
A people I have not known shall serve me.
[44] As soon as they hear of me they obey me;
The foreigners submit to me. [45] The foreigners fade away,
And come frightened from their hideouts.
Psalms 18:43-45.

Before leaving Nigeria, the Lord showed me in a vision that I would minister to Indians. I took no thought of it because I had limited exposure to Indians. Nathan, a family friend with whom we occasionally exchanged visits, was the only Indian I knew. After the church started in the USA, I was on a visit to Maryland (MD) when I received a call from an Indian man named Abba. He asked that I come to pray for him and gave me his address in Woonsocket, RI. I promised to visit him, and after returning from MD, I did. Getting there, I met a young couple. They had a young child. I asked the man what he wanted me to pray about, and he said that he had a back problem that had persisted for three years. He said that he could not bend down.

I went through some Scriptures to build his faith and prayed for him. Then I asked him to bend, and he did without any back pain. We rejoiced about what the Lord did. I asked for some oil to anoint him and his family, but the only oil available was in the saucepan on the stove. With their permission, I took some of the oil, laid my hand on the wife's head, and she was slain in the Spirit. I was amazed because I did not expect anything like that at all. I was full of joy to see the wonders of God. I then anointed the husband and the little girl. After spending a little time with them, I left.

A week later, Abba called me to say that his back problem had returned and that he could not bend down anymore. I asked him, "Were you healed the day I prayed for you?" He said that he was, and I asked again, "Did I give you medication for your healing?" He said, "No." Then I asked, "If you were healed without any medication when I prayed for you, how can the back problem return?" I told him that the devil was trying to rob him of his miracle. I said that he should affirm his healing and command the devil to remove his hand from his back. Immediately he did; he was restored.

Few weeks later, Abba called me and said that he would gather Indians living in the state so that I could minister to them. From that time, he gathered them, and I ministered the word of God to them. Shaker, another Indian brother, joined the effort, and we held meetings all over Massachusetts in Framingham, Burlington, Billerica, Arlington, Worcester, Natick, Boston, and other places.

Remembering the vision that I would minister to Indians, I asked Abba one day how he got my contact. He told me that he got it from the Yellow Pages. What the Lord said, He did all by Himself. Of all the churches and pastors listed in the Yellow Pages, in order to fulfill His word, the Lord directed a total stranger who was an Indian to pick my name, contact me, and receive the miracle that would inspire him to gather for me the people the Lord wanted me to minister to. What a mighty God we have. Indeed, nothing is too hard for Him.

The Lord did many miracles, signs, and wonders among the Indians. Some of them are as follows:

Miracle Baby
At a gathering in Natick, after ministering, I decided to pray for the attendees individually. I came to a man, and a lady was sitting beside him. I asked him what he wanted us to pray about. He said that he needed a car. I then asked him, "Who is this by your side? Is she your sister?" He said, "No,

she is my wife." Then I asked him, "How long have you been married?" He said, "Eight years." Then I said, "It is not a car that you need but a child. By this time next year, you will have a son in the name of Jesus Christ." Ten months later, they had a son, and the Lord still gave them the car that I didn't pray about.

A Demon-Possessed Woman Delivered
About eighteen months after the birth of their son, a woman traveled to Pakistan but came back demon-possessed. The husband called me at 10pm one night and told me that the person who came back from Pakistan was not his wife because she was demon-possessed. That night, he said that he would like to bring her for deliverance. I told him that, being too late, he should bring her the following morning. When they came, the woman did not speak. Whenever I looked at her, she would avoid my gaze by putting her face down. When I commanded in the name of Jesus that the demon should come out of her, she began to manifest. Though a tiny woman, her husband, who was far bigger than she, could not restrain her. I kept my distance because I knew that no physical power could contain her. When the demon left her, she spoke and said, "I am myself now." She was free, and they returned home rejoicing.

A Ten Year Old Boy Deaf In One Ear Was Healed
One Sunday, a woman who was a member of the Indian Ministry came from Billerica to Providence to attend our church service. After the service, she said, "Pastor Femi, I know that if you pray for my son, he will be healed." We ministered many times in her house in Billerica and never noticed anything wrong with her son. So I asked her what was wrong with him, and she said that he was deaf in one ear. I prayed for the boy, and after praying, I counted numerals while walking away from him. He heard and repeated the numbers. Again, I spoke while walking away from him, but he did not hear the words. I told the woman that her son's

healing had started and would be perfected. The following Sunday, the woman returned with joy because her son was perfectly healed. In her testimony, she told us that her son was born at Massachusetts General Hospital with that condition. She also said that the doctors told her there was no solution and that if the boy was exposed to noise, he would go totally deaf. She was overjoyed and said that since his healing, even when she whispered from far away, her son could hear.

The Holy Spirit Helped A Software Engineer
The woman whose son was healed had a brother who had a master's degree in software engineering and worked at a bank in New York. She called and told me one Sunday that her brother had problems and needed prayers. I asked her to tell her brother to call me. The brother called me that evening and told me that he had written a software program for his bank, but it did not work despite all his efforts. He said that he received an ultimatum that if the program failed to work by Monday, he would be fired. I had met him once before in his sister's house and knew that he was a Christian, but I asked him, "Are you a Christian?" After affirming that he was, I asked him again, "Don't you know that the Holy Spirit can write the program?" He sounded puzzled. I assured him that all he needed was the help of the Holy Spirit, and I prayed with him. I then told him that all it would cost him was a sleepless night since the program had to work the following morning. I also told him that before working on the program, he should simply say, "Holy Spirit, I am ready now; teach me." He did, worked on the software program that night, and at the bank the following morning, the program worked.

The teaching ministry of the Holy Spirit is of great benefit to us. Jesus Christ said, ***"But the Helper, the Holy Spirit, whom the Father will send in My name, <u>He will teach you all things</u>, and bring to your remembrance all things that I*** *said to you."* John 14:26. The Holy Spirit will teach us all things. All things mean all things. There is nothing the Holy Spirit cannot teach us. He is a software engineer, doctor, physicist, mathematician, chemist, pharmacist, businessman, artist, carpenter, cook, landscaper, tailor, plumber, etc.

Injustice Of 15 Years Was Terminated
A young Indian man approached and told me in a very sad tone how his family was being humiliated and shamed in India. He came from a family of timber merchants, but government interference bankrupted the business. The suit filed by his family for compensation was prolonged by the government and their condition worsened. Moved by the young man's concern for his family, we prayed and asked the Lord to give judgment in their favor based on Daniel 7:21-22. The suit was expedited, and three months after our prayer, judgment was given in favor of his family. The Lord ended their shame and reproach.

Operations Of The Excellent Spirit Of God
At one of the services in Arlington, MA, a woman said that her daughter was struggling in school with poor grades. As I assured the young girl, who was in high school, that the Lord would give her better grades, she wept. I comforted her and then laid hands on her head and prayed that the Lord would release the same excellent Spirit He gave Daniel and his friends on her, so that her performance in her studies might bring glory to God. Not long after, her grades improved significantly, and she later secured admission to a prestigious university in Massachusetts.

Spirit Of Suicide Cast Out
I received an urgent call from Shaker, the coordinator of the Indian ministry, that the wife of one of the brothers called in panic, saying that her husband was about to commit suicide. Shaker said that he was driving to Billerica to the brother's house and asked that I join him there. I dropped all

79

engagements, and in the company of Rick Roderick, drove to Billerica. There was a very heavy downpour that slowed our journey, and we got there at 10pm. Shaker and his wife were already there. The man who was threatening to commit suicide appeared to be paranoid. I did not know what to do. In desperation, I asked the Holy Spirit in my mind, "Lord, what do you want me to do?" Then He said, "Just praise Me." I told the people that we should just praise the Lord. As we began to praise the Lord, to our amazement, the brother joined us and started praising the Lord as if nothing had happened! I did not have to say anything. I did not counsel or try to persuade him against committing suicide. The Lord Himself touched him as we praised Him! The brother went on to have a wonderful career in a bank in New York as a software engineer. My wife and I visited them many times. They are doing very well to the glory of God.

Again, the Lord never ceases to respond to our cry. If we follow His counsel, we will experience deliverance without sweat. Turning to the Lord, especially in difficult times, is the way out of disaster. Praising God in times of trouble is an exercise of faith and confidence in the Almighty God. Praise relies on the omniscience and omnipotence of God. God is aroused to act as we praise Him. This is consistent with what the Lord told me at the beginning of our ministry, saying, *"Your ministry must be built on worship and the Word of God."* God confirmed that truth that day in Billerica, MA. Glory to the Lord God Almighty, who does wonderful things.

Barrenness Terminated
At one of the meetings in Ashland, MA, the mother of one of the brothers told me that her daughter, a doctor who was married to a doctor, was unable to have a child after many years of marriage. I prayed with her. The daughter, who lived in New York, came to one of our meetings in her brother's house in Medford, MA, and I prayed with her again. Not long after, she became pregnant and had a son.

CHAPTER ELEVEN

MIRACLES IN MARYLAND

And these signs will follow those who believe: In My name they will cast out demons; they will speak with new tongues; [18] they will take up serpents; and if they drink anything deadly, it will by no means hurt them; they will lay hands on the sick, and they will recover."
Mark 16:17-18.

The Problems Of Life Disappeared
I was in Maryland to worship at Newness of Life Bible Church, where Bishop Mills was the pastor. Bishop Mills asked me to minister, and after I did, I prayed with the people individually. I laid hands on some of them. Some months later, a woman who was an elder at the church came to give her testimony in our church in Providence. In her testimony, she said, "Pastor Femi, when you stood before me in Maryland, you said, 'By the time I lay my hands on you, all the problems of your life will disappear.'" I did not remember ever saying such a thing. Then I asked her what happened, and she said that all the problems of her life disappeared. She said that after thirteen years without a promotion, the bank had just promoted her. She said that in her fifty years of life, she had never received any proposal for marriage but had just received one and would be getting married in a few months.

Miraculous Bulk Sale
I accompanied my friend to an apartment to buy some shirts. The vendor had a reputable men's clothing chain store that gave him leftover clothes at a huge discount. The stock of clothes grew over the years. His large three-bedroom apartment was stacked full of suits, pants, shirts, and jeans. Only the resident's bed and kitchen were free. The clothes were not arranged in order. It took my friend a long time to

find the shirts he liked. After I drew the man's attention to the inefficiencies of his business model, he said that he could not afford to rent a store and didn't know what to do. His living condition was frustrating, to say the least.

He also complained about a lady who was sleeping in his bed while he used the couch. According to him, the lady never accepted good counsel but always brought trouble upon herself and had to be rescued often. I told him that if we prayed, the Lord would send somebody to buy the clothes in bulk and also deliver him from the compromising position he found himself in with the lady in his apartment. Having obtained his consent, I filled a basin with water and prayed, saying, "This is no longer water but the blood of Jesus in Jesus' name." Using "the blood of Jesus," I sprinkled the stock and his apartment. Three weeks later, the man called to say that the lady left his apartment on the same day that we prayed. He also said that someone bought the whole stock of clothes for cash and that his apartment is no longer filled with goods.

Shipping Business Established
My friend, who had been in the car business for decades, was invited to attend a meeting by the shippers he used to ship vehicles to Nigeria. He asked me to accompany him. The event was well attended, mostly by West African clients. The shippers spoke to them about new procedures for shipping. At the end of the meeting, people mingled while having snacks that were provided by the shipping company. I thought of the presenter's speech, and on the way home, I was inspired to tell my friend that he didn't need to rely on the shippers but could establish a shipping company himself. I told him not to ignore it but to work on the idea. Then the Lord connected him and two other partners with a person who had a shipping license. They obtained their own shipping license three years later and now have a flourishing shipping company.

Car Problem Resolved
On one of my visits to Maryland, my friend asked me to bless a new warehouse they had recently acquired for their shipping business. After blessing the warehouse, a man standing nearby who heard us pray approached me. He told me that he had bought a car that would not work. He said that three mechanics had worked on the car but could not fix it. He had been spending money, but the car was not fixed. As he spoke, I saw a fourth mechanic struggling to fix the car. I walked to the car, laid my hand on it, and declared that the car was made whole and that he would not need to spend any additional money on it. Within minutes, the car worked perfectly. The following day, at my friend's church, the man, who was a member of the church, gave a testimony about the car and how it worked perfectly after we prayed.

Haulage Business
After praying over the car, another person asked that I pray over the truck which he had recently acquired for his haulage business. I prayed and declared that he would acquire more trucks and employ workers to drive for him. He gave me an offering of one hundred dollars. Less than a year later, my friend confirmed that the man had acquired a fleet of trucks and had drivers working for him. The Lord established His word.

Finnancial Provision
On a trip to Maryland, I took only fifty dollars with me. I also had in my wallet a check for five hundred dollars that I did not have time to deposit. Upon getting to Maryland, I learned that there was a three-dayrevival in my friend's church. I told him that if he had informed me, I would have come with money for the offering. On the first day of the revival, I decided that I would give twenty dollars, give twenty dollars the second day, and the remaining ten dollars on the third day. However, on the first day, the Lord asked me to give the fifty dollars as an offering, and I did.

It was the second day that we went to pray at my friend's warehouse, over the car and the truck for the haulage business. That evening, at the church, the Lord asked me to give the one-hundred-dollar offering that I received from the truck owner, and I did. On the last day of the revival, the Lord asked me to endorse the five hundred dollar check in my pocket to the church, and I did.

The next day, I received a call from Bob Padgett - an elderly friend and mentor - asking me to visit him in Virginia before returning to Providence. He said that he had arranged that I minister to some people over dinner. I arrived at Bob Padgett's house a little before dinner. He was with two people: his son and his wife. We talked briefly, and as we went to the dinner table, one of the two people slipped a twenty dollar bill into my hand, and I thanked her. After dinner, I bid them goodbye. He, his wife, and son walked with me to the car. The son handed me an envelope and I thanked him. I found later that it contained one thousand three hundred dollars - exactly double the offerings that I gave at the revival! I showed the money to my friend explaining how the Lord had led me to give all that I had, totaling six hundred and fifty dollars at the revival. The Lord even gave me twenty dollars extra through one of the two people at the dinner!

Here again is another example of how God blesses us when we obey His word. At the time I gave the money that I had at His instructions, I just obeyed. I had no idea that I would receive any money. But the Lord graciously prepared an envelope for me without my knowledge. When we refuse to do what the Lord tells us to do, we deny ourselves the blessings He reserves for us. Obedience is the key to our walking in the blessing of the Lord.

Emaciating Man Healed
On another trip to Maryland, we went to get coffee on our return journey by road to Providence. At the coffee shop, my friend called a man and asked him to meet us at the shop. On arrival, my friend told me to pray for the man. Without asking any questions, I prayed for him, and we left. The man, who was a scientist, later gave a testimony of how the Lord healed him. He said that he was plagued with a high body temperature and was losing weight rapidly. Many medical investigations revealed nothing. His condition deteriorated, and he talked with his wife about putting his house in order before his death. When giving his testimony, he said that the day we prayed, the high body temperature ceased, and he began to gain weight. God delivered him from the strange ailment that several medical examinations could not reveal.

A Young Man's Life Was Transformed.
On another visit to Maryland, I was in my friend's office when a young man came to see him. Before leaving, my friend asked me to pray for the young man, and I did. The Lord led me to speak prophetic words about his life and business. The Lord used that prayer to transform the young man's life. Immediately after, the struggle with his co-tenant ceased. His landlord offered him a new property at a cheaper rent. He had ample space for his business, and he sublet the unused space for thrice his monthly rent for the property. His business grew. When the lease of his previous co-tenant expired in the adjoining building, the landlord offered him the lease. In his testimony, he said that after the prayer, it was as if the Lord opened the window of heaven over his life. He prospered in all things and never stopped praising God for the miraculous turnaround that he received from the Lord.

CHAPTER TWELVE

OTHER WONDERFUL WORKS OF GOD

Many, O LORD my God, are your wonderful works
Which you have done; And your thoughts toward us cannot
be recounted to you in order; If I would declare and speak
of them, They are more than can be numbered.
Psalms 40:5.

God Overturned Shame

A sister in the church asked me to pray over her friend's store. I went to the store, and as I prayed, the daughter of the store owner came in. I turned abruptly to the daughter and began to pray for her. When I finished praying, the sister who invited me to the store was troubled. She told me that her friend would not believe that she did not tell me about her life and her daughter because I was praying and making declarations about their exact problems. I told her not to worry since she did not tell me anything about them. The friend started attending the church, and over the years, the daughter who was using drugs at the time I visited her mother's store was fully restored. The Lord turned her life around. She went back to school and graduated as an RN - Registered Nurse.

God Gave Us A Car

One of our church members was driving me home in my car one evening, and he said that the vehicle was not running smoothly. Then I said, *"The Lord will have to give us a new vehicle then."* A few weeks later, I received a call from my realtor friend, and he asked me to come and collect a car for my use - a 1998 Volvo S70 that served us for a few years.

A Boy Came Out Of Coma

One evening, a member of the church visited us in the company of her daughter and her son. After spending time

86

with us, they bid us goodbye, and I decided to see them off. On the staircase, the daughter turned around and asked me to pray for her friend who was in a coma. I asked her if her friend was a boy or a girl, and she said that he was a boy. She also said that her classmates and their teacher were concerned for him. When I asked how long her friend had been in a coma, she said it had been weeks. I told her to pray, and she did. Without praying, I was led by the Lord to say, "When you get to school tomorrow, go and tell your teacher that your pastor said your friend would come out of the coma today." I told her not to forget, and she promised she wouldn't. The following morning, she went and told her teacher what I said, and after she did, her friend came out of the coma before noon.

Criminal Case Plea Bargain

A member of our church had a serious criminal case. He was charged with mayhem, which carried a sentence of up to twenty years in prison. I had warned him before to steer clear of trouble. I was worried, but we prayed and asked the Lord for forgiveness. I asked the Lord to be the judge in the case and grant favor to his son. I attended the court daily, praying during the proceedings and checking with the lawyer about the tempo of the case. A day before the verdict, the Lord told me that He would deliver the young man in stages, and I told him. On the day of the verdict, there was a hung jury. The prosecuting counsel was forced to offer him a plea bargain of five years' probation and that the charges would be expunged at the end of five years. The lawyer, convinced that the plea bargain was very appropriate, asked his client to take it.

On our way home, thinking he would have a better verdict, he insisted that he desired a retrial. I told him that if he went to trial again, he would lose and go to prison. Insisting that his lawyer should go back to trial, I offered to accompany him to hear what his lawyer would say. The lawyer, in my presence, told him that if the case went to trial again, he

87

would lose and go to prison. He explained that the prosecutor had to offer the plea bargain because during the trial, he made an error that he would not make again in a new trial. After we left the lawyer, I reminded him that the Lord said that He would deliver him in stages and that he should be grateful for the deliverance he has received from God.

State Laws Changed For Our Children's College Tuition
While in high school, we were preoccupied with how we would pay our children's college tuition. The fees were very high, and we persuaded our older son to enroll in a community college. That demoralized him, but that year the state passed a bill that allowed all residents of the state to qualify for in-state tuition. This was a big relief.

College Tuition Funded Through Credit Card
I went to a local clothing store to purchase some items. At the checkout counter, I wrote a check for my purchase. The counter clerk asked me if I would like to open an account. Thinking it was an account to track my purchases, I consented. She completed a form, had me sign it, and went into a corner room with it. She came back to tell me that an official would like to speak to me on the phone. The person on the other end said that he could not approve a store credit card for me. I told him that I was not applying for a store credit card because I had already issued a check for my purchase. I let him know that I thought the account was to track my purchases. Hearing that, he said, "I will approve a credit card of three hundred dollars for you." I came out to tell the counter clerk that I did not understand that she was making a store credit card application for me.

Over the years, my credit improved significantly, and other credit cards were approved for me. When our sons were in college, at the time to pay their tuition, I would receive a credit card offer in the mail for thousands of dollars for twelve, fifteen, eighteen, and twenty-one months with zero interest. Through these credit card offers, we were able to fund our children's college tuition, which we later paid off conveniently without any stress.

A Recalcitrant Tenant Apologized

I was passing by when I heard one of our members speaking to another about her plight with a tenant. She obtained a judgment in court against her tenant. To frustrate her, the tenant did not vacate but locked the apartment, took the keys, and went away. After many months, she went back to court and was told that she should put the tenant's properties in storage if she wanted to secure her apartment. Upon hearing this, I was furious and said that she would do no such thing. I said that we would pray and the tenant would pack her things with her own hands. A few days later, I went to the premises with my wife, and we prayed. I put some water in a basin and declared, "This is no longer water but the blood of Jesus, in Jesus' name." I sprinkled the door to the apartment with the blood of Jesus and decreed by the inspiration of the Holy Spirit that before the end of the week, the tenant would return, pack her belongings, apologize, and return the keys. To confirm His word, the Lord told me that as I laid hands on the landlady, the Spirit of God would come upon her in power. I did not tell her because I didn't want it to be suggestive. I just laid hands on her, and the Spirit of the Lord came upon her in power, as the Lord said. Then I told her what the Lord said before I laid hands on her. The next day, the tenant did exactly what I decreed by the inspiration of the Lord. She returned, packed her belongings, apologized, and returned the keys to the landlady. The apartment was cleaned and rented to a new tenant shortly after.

Loan Was Waived After Short Sale of House

Another time, I heard the same lady thanking God for being able to pay the mortgage for her second house, even when the tenants were not paying their rent. I interrupted her and said that paying the mortgage and not getting rent is not the

89

will of God for her. I explained that the enemy was robbing her of her blessing. It was a time of glut, and most houses were in foreclosure. I told her that if she was willing to let go of the house, we would pray, and it would be sold. She said that the mortgaged value of the house was far higher than the market value. She was not even sure that anyone would buy the house because of the prevailing housing market situation. Anyhow, we went to pray around the building because we could not enter the premises, as that would mean a violation of the tenants' privacy. The house was sold less than three months after.

The house sold for one hundred and fifty thousand dollars below its mortgaged value. When she told me that the bank insisted that she should pay the shortfall, I asked her, "Did you not give back the same house you bought from them?" When she said that she did, I declared that she owed the bank nothing. A few weeks later, she told me that a bank official was insisting that she should agree to payment terms for the one hundred and fifty thousand dollars. I told her that she would not, and that if the bank official would not relent, he would be fired, and a new person who would work with her would take his place. Not long after, the man was fired, and the woman who replaced him settled for thirty-five dollars.

A Couple Was Blessed With A Son
We met a couple who had a ten year old daughter, and she was their only child. We sometimes visit them, and one day I was inspired to ask the husband if they wanted more children. He said they would like to have another child. Assuring him that the Lord would bless him and his wife with another child, I prayed. The man started attending our church. A few months later, his wife became pregnant. When she went for an ante-natal visit one day, her doctor was not on duty, and a new doctor was assigned to attend to her. The doctor, apparently dissatisfied with examining her, violently pushed her hand into her and damaged her placenta. This resulted in

the loss of the baby. We prayed again, and within a couple of months, she was pregnant. The pregnancy progressed very well, but at about eight months, she was involved in an accident in which her vehicle flipped several times, but the Lord preserved her and the baby. She gave birth to a very healthy boy not long after. The Lord always perfects all that concerns us.

Object Moving In The Body Disappeared
A few weeks after a couple came to church, I paid them a visit. The man had gone out before my arrival. During my discussion with the lady, I found that she was not married to the man, and I encouraged her to live by the word of God. While talking to her, I observed that she was moving her body strangely. When I asked her why, she said that an object moving in her body was giving her pain. She was moving to mimic the movement of the object in her body. I prayed for her and left. In the meantime, the Lord gave me a song - *"You are the Lord, that is your name"* - and told me that it is a deliverance song. One day, while visiting the lady, I prayed into oil and asked that she anoint herself regularly with it. I also taught her the song that the Lord gave me and asked her to sing it for her deliverance.

A few weeks later, the lady gave a testimony in tears. She said that the object moving in her body had disappeared. For the first time in years, she no longer had pain. She said that prior to coming to the church, she had gone to Nigeria to seek help, but to no avail, and that what she went to seek in Nigeria, the Lord brought to her doorstep. We arranged for her to move in with one of the women in the church to avoid the sinful lifestyle with the man.

An Enviable Church Building
At the beginning of our ministry, I wrote to many people asking that they make a donation toward the purchase of our church building. One of the letters was received by Bob

Padgett, an elderly friend and mentor in Virginia. He wrote back to tell me that I should not solicit money for the church building but that I should concentrate on building the body of Christ. He said that the Lord would provide us a building at the right time. Before receiving his letter, one person had already sent us a check. I sent back the check and wrote to the people who received our first letter, telling them to ignore our request for donations. I then focused on building the body of Christ, as Bob suggested. I frequently separate myself to seek the face of the Lord. One of those days, I was at the Best Western Hotel in Seekonk, MA, for three days. On the last day of my prayer, I said, "Lord, I have consecrated myself and have been in your presence for the past three days. What do you say?" Then, the Lord said, "I will give you an enviable place where the ministries will be established."

After receiving the word of the Lord, I announced to the church that we should start looking for a church building. We saw many buildings that we liked, but at the last minute, it would not go through. I always told the church that we must not be desperate and that the Lord would give us the right building. There was an eleven thousand square-foot building that we all loved. The owner was willing to hold the mortgage. He asked for seven hundred thousand dollars, but our agent offered four hundred thousand dollars. The owner said that he felt insulted and would not discuss it further. We saw another building with twelve thousand square feet on two floors for three hundred and fifty thousand dollars, but the city would not approve it for a church.

On the internet, we saw a building of fourteen thousand square feet on three floors. After going to see the building, and as I was entering my apartment, I heard the Lord say, "Offer them one hundred thousand dollars cash." I called our agent, and he made the offer. The offer was accepted within one hour. We signed a purchase/sale agreement and had ninety days for due diligence. First, we did not have one hundred thousand dollars in cash. Secondly, I felt that if the seller was willing to accept one hundred thousand dollars, there must be something wrong with the building. Thirdly, I contacted a lawyer who, upon inspecting the building, said that he would get it for us for ten thousand dollars!

Suspecting that something was wrong with the building, I brought several experts to inspect it. The last one, who was a structural engineer, took me through the building to show me the quality and strength of the structure. He told me that the sprinkler system and the steel staircase were each worth more than one hundred thousand dollars. He showed me the stone foundation of the building and finally said, "They don't build like this anymore." Our lawyer went on vacation and did not get back to me. I wasted time trying to find the flaws in the building, and by the time I was persuaded otherwise, the due diligence period was over.

Knowing that we could lose the building, I asked the Lord for forgiveness for thinking that a man would give me for ten thousand dollars what He said that He would give us for one hundred thousand dollars. I also repented for thinking that there was something wrong with the gift of God. Then the Lord said, "What I have reserved for you in Christ, I will put in your hand," and I was greatly relieved. The due diligence period having expired, the owners insisted that they would not sell the building for less than one hundred and ten thousand dollars. Our lawyer said he would sue them, but knowing that it may jeopardize the purchase, I told him not to. We finally paid one hundred and ten thousand dollars for the building. The Lord, being humorous, made us pay ten thousand dollars for thinking that our lawyer could do a better job than He.

The building was admired by all. The price was unbelievable. The Lord provided. We paid cash as He said, and He gave us an enviable place as He had said.

The Lord Gave Us A House

While working on the church building, our landlord gave us a quit notice for a minor misunderstanding. We looked for a new apartment but could not find any. The treasurer of our church advised that we consider buying a house, but I was not ready for the distraction of house maintenance, and I told him so. He told me to look around with his agent just to see what is available even if we would not buy. We found a house that was only eight years old, and the mortgage was only three hundred dollars more than our monthly rent! The house was one mile from the church. We moved into the house two weeks after we purchased the church building.

A Paralyzed Girl Healed

I was asked by one of our members to visit the hospital and pray for his niece. I got to the hospital to find that the girl had undergone a procedure that left her paralyzed from her neck down. I prayed and told her that she would walk again. I visited her at home regularly after she left the hospital to pray and inspire her. She was always in bed, and I told her that I would dance with her to glorify God for her healing. Later, she used a wheelchair, but one day during church service, she walked in with her parents. We praised the Lord, and I danced with her as I promised, rejoicing for what the Lord had done.

Firing Of A Legal Director

The treasurer of our church provided accounting services as a contractor for a reputable and large chain store. Desiring to have him as a full-time staff member, the company decided to file for him, thereby regularizing his immigration status, but the legal director opposed it. The treasurer, worried about the situation, spoke to me, and we prayed. The end of his contract was fast approaching, but the legal director did not change her mind. Knowing that the company would let him go if the filing was not done before the expiration of his contract, I decreed that if the legal director refused to file his papers, and his services were consequently terminated, the legal director would be fired, and he would be re-engaged. That was exactly what happened. The legal director was fired. He was recalled and given his job back. The company filed for the regularization of his immigration status. Years later, he retired from the job.

Firing Of A Departmental Head In Australia
An elder brother of one of our members living in Australia called to inform me of the pressures and threats that he was receiving from his supervisor at work. He was afraid that he could be fired at any time despite his diligence and hard work because the supervisor was biased against him. We prayed many times, but the threat grew worse. Filled with anxiety, his work began to suffer. He was sure that he would be terminated at any moment. Then, in anger, I declared that if his supervisor did not stop threatening him, he would be fired and someone else would be appointed as his supervisor. A few months later, that supervisor was fired. A new person was appointed as his supervisor. The new supervisor liked his work ethic. His job was secure, and within a year, he was promoted, and he continued to flourish in the company.

Purchases Of Things For Almost Nothing
When I got to the United States, I had only five hundred dollars that I left in an account during my previous visits. The church did not give me any stipend for many months. My friend had to persuade the church before they gave me a monthly stipend of $200. After many months, he spoke to the church, and my stipend was increased to $400. It took almost two years before the church increased my stipend to $500 a month. That was my monthly stipend until I returned to Nigeria in 2002. In the four years that I was in the United

States, I did no other work because the Lord told me that my ministry must be full-time.

That low income did not allow me to get the things I needed. I often bought used clothes at the thrift store. When I returned to the United States in 2004, I was put back on $500 a month. My income was increased to one thousand dollars when my family joined me in 2006. I never took it upon myself to determine my income. My income did not improve until we started our own ministry. The elders of the church fixed my income from the inception of my ministry. I was able to buy a few shirts, shorts, and shoes for myself, but one day the Lord told me to pack them in a box and take them to Winners Chapel in New York, and I did. As I got out of the van, carried the box, and walked to the entrance of the church in New York, I heard a song in my spirit: *"You raised me up."* I was very thankful to God for this song. I dropped the box, spoke with the pastor, and drove back to Providence.

Since then, I noticed that my purchases from reputable stores were at a fraction of their values. I got $120 pants for $19. I got $45 shirts for $13. I got very expensive shoes for less than twenty dollars. I got $450 winter coats for $19. I got $45 and $55 ties for $5 and $8. From one of them, I ordered clothes, and when I went to pick them up at their store, a pant that I did not order was included in my consignment. When I told the store manager that I did not order the pants, he insisted it was part of my consignment. I took delivery of the pants with the intention of checking the record of my online order to ascertain whether I ordered it or not. When I confirmed that I did not order the pants, I took it back to the store a few days later. At the store, I told the store manager that I did not order the pants and was returning it. I also said that I liked the pants and would buy it if the price was affordable. After checking his computer, he told me the price was $25. While paying for the pants, he looked at me and said, "Do you know how much this pants normally costs?" I said I didn't, and he said that the original price was $250. I was taken aback because I knew that the Lord was giving me the pants for 10% of its cost.

As I drove back home, I asked the Lord, "What have I done to deserve this?" At that time, the Lord reminded me of the time when I was wearing used clothes from the thrift store, serving without discouragement, complaining, or grumbling. I was amazed because the Lord remembered that.

My wardrobe of expensive clothes, ties, and shoes cost me only a fraction of their value. The Lord gave me those things at a fifth, a tenth, or less of their value. The Lord consistently teaches us His principles through the instructions He gives us. If we are willing and obedient, indeed we will eat the good of the land, as Isaiah 1:19 says. If we obey and serve Him, we will spend our days in prosperity and our years in pleasure, as Job 36:11 says.

God stuns unbelievers and makes them envious of His blessings on our lives. This was revealed one day when I went to a hospital in Attleboro, MA, to pray for one of our members. I wore simple pants, a shirt, and shoes. But one of the nurses, murmuring, spoke against me, saying, "They call themselves pastors but wear expensive things." Though expensive, the total cost to me of what I wore was less than $100. Hearing what she said, I gave glory to the Almighty God who gave me those things for a pittance.

The Lord Gave Us A Second Church Building
In the year 2019, the Lord began to lay on my heart to acquire another building. Sometime in 2021, I decided to act on the word of the Lord. I was with Pastor Akin, who came to visit us from Togo, when I saw a church building online for sale in Woonsocket, RI. Pastor Akin desired to go with me to see the building but could not because his bus trip to New York was in fifteen minutes. I drove him to the bus

97

station, which was about five minutes away, and promised that I would give him feedback after inspecting the building.

Immediately after dropping off Pastor Akin, I decided to go see the building, but the Lord told me not to go. I wrestled with this because the building looked big, and the price was reasonable. It had an adjoining minister's residence and good parking. So we began the search for a church building, but not finding any, I went to see the building in Woonsocket. The five or six other buildings we inspected were inadequate, and we finally decided to suspend the search.

Before commencing our search, I looked for the real estate agent who assisted us in acquiring our first property but could not find him. The man who introduced him to us said that he had lost contact with him. He recommended another person who worked tirelessly to find us a place but without success. A few days after the decision to postpone our search, I went online and found a property for sale in Providence. It was a building that I had always loved. I had gone inside it once before to admire it. The listing agent for the property was the man who assisted us in acquiring our first property! I called him, and after we exchanged pleasantries, but before I asked about the property, he said, "Pastor Femi, I have a property listed in Providence. If you are free, I can show it to you tomorrow at 10 a.m." I confirmed that I was calling about the property and that I would meet with him at 10 a.m.

I quickly mobilized the members who were available, and we went to see the building. The Mormon church, which was the owner, had thoroughly refurbished the building. It was fully equipped. In the basement was a fully functioning baptistery. It had many well-maintained and neat classrooms. We were excited about the building. We made an offer, and the offer was accepted. We closed on the purchase in April 2022. It was fourteen thousand square feet of space on three floors. It had two overflow areas that we used to host seminars, baby showers, naming ceremonies, and other celebrations. We had an elaborate parking space and a plot of land opposite the building that we also use for parking. Though the first building was truly enviable, the second is even more enviable. As Psalm 84:11 says, *"For the LORD God is a sun and shield; The LORD will give grace and glory; No good thing will He withhold from those who walk uprightly."* The Lord also told me that we should not sell the buildings that He gives to us. I don't know if He would change that in the future.

After acquiring the building, because of its greatness, I began to feel that I might have allowed my flesh and pride to push me into getting it. I had that feeling for months until the Lord spoke to me from Isaiah 28:29 which says, *"This also comes from the LORD of hosts, who is wonderful in counsel and excellent in guidance".* Then I had peace, knowing that the building came from the Lord of hosts through His wonderful counsel and excellent work.

The Lord Gave Me Another Car
A brother visited me one day and said that the transmission of his car had packed up. I decided to lend him my Volvo car to ease his commute. A few weeks later, the Lord laid on my heart to give him the car, and I did. So, I borrowed the Honda Odyssey, which I had given to the church as a gift a few years back. A Christian sister came to me a few weeks later and said that if I continued using the van, people might think that I took it back. I told her that the pastor and the van belong to the church and that I have the right to use the van while looking to buy a car.

I finally decided to buy a Chrysler van, but in a dream a few days after my decision, I saw a beautiful Mercedes ML 350. I was puzzled, wondering if that was the car the Lord wanted me to have. I browsed online looking for a car to buy, but I did not find what I liked. The Christian sister visited again and offered me a check for five thousand dollars as a deposit for a car. I was reluctant to take the check, not being sure if the husband was aware of it. When I asked, she confirmed that it was a joint decision with her husband. The couple took me to a car dealership, but I did not find the right car. I went back on my computer only to find that I had not closed the page that I had browsed. So, I continued my search on the same website, and two pages later, I found the Mercedes ML 350 that the Lord showed me in my dream.

The following day, I went to the dealership, made a deposit, and agreed to pick up the car the next day. The couple who gave me the deposit offered to drive me to the dealership to pick up the car. When I signed the papers and received the keys, the sister went on her knees, asking that they pay the monthly car note. Not accepting my protest, I acquiesced. She sent me the payment faithfully, but I was also making payments, and the vehicle was fully paid off in 24 months instead of sixty months. When she gave me another payment and I told her that she didn't need to because the vehicle was fully paid, she was surprised.

My experience with the purchase of the church buildings, our own house, and the Mercedes ML 350 confirmed that God does exceedingly abundantly above all that we ask or think - Ephesians 3:20. None of the buildings we wanted to buy compared with those that the Lord gave us. I would have bought the Chrysler van if the Lord had not shown me the Mercedes. If we hurriedly make decisions without His input, we will acquire or get what is inferior to what our Father wants for us. The experience taught me that we must never be desperate for anything. When we patiently wait and allow Him to give us what He has for us, God is glorified. Our choice will always be inferior to that of God.

A New York Marriage Restored

Pastor Akin visited us on one of his trips from Togo for a few days. One of those days, he was talking to a woman on the phone and abruptly gave me the phone and said, "Daddy, please pray for this woman who has a problem in her marriage." I took the phone and prayed for her. After the prayer, I was inspired to tell her that she should go and prepare right away her husband's favorite meal, set the table, and let her husband eat when he comes home. When I gave the phone back to Pastor Akin, he screamed, saying, "Daddy, how do you know? The woman is from a wealthy family. She has a good job earning a six figure salary, but she could not cook. Though she always ordered very good food for her husband at her own expense, the husband is not pleased because he wants the food prepared by his wife. That is the exact problem with their marriage." I told Pastor Akin that I didn't know but simply told her what the Lord inspired me to say. That day, immediately after the prayer, we gathered that the woman went to her mother-in-law and asked her to teach her how to cook her husband's favorite meal. Working together with her mother-in-law, she prepared the food and brought it home, set the table, and asked her husband to eat. When the husband saw and ate the food, hostility disappeared, and their marriage was saved.

Most often, marriage problems are caused by simple things that can be resolved if we allow the Holy Spirit to guide us. Remember that by waiting until the husband came home and embracing him as the Lord instructed, the marriage of the woman in the upper room on page 65 of this book was restored. This is another example of how simply the Lord solves marital problems when we take them to Him in prayer and, with an open heart, follow His instructions.

A Scholarship For Our Son

In September 2021, our son David won an 80% scholarship to study at Babson College, the most prominent college for entrepreneurial studies in the United States. The scholarship was newly endowed, and he was the first beneficiary. The scholarship was for an MBA in entrepreneurial studies, which would commence that September. We were glad and rejoiced in the kindness and goodness of God. A few weeks after the news, I was in my office searching for a notebook that I would use for a journal. I found one that contained a few pages of notes. I decided to use the notebook, but before using it, I looked through it. I was surprised to see a prayer that I recorded 12 years earlier asking the Lord to give David a scholarship to study in the United States. I had no clue that I had ever prayed on the subject. I was reminded of the prayer for dark suits that I also forgot but which the Lord answered. God is awesome. His goodness towards us is amazing. He neither forgets nor denies our requests. God hears and answers our prayers in His own time because He makes all things beautiful in His own time.

Issue of Blood Dried Up
A lady asked that I pray with her one afternoon, and without asking about what she wanted to pray for, I prayed for her. She said a few days later that when she asked me to pray for her, she had had an issue of blood for some time. She said that she was weak, pale, and without any relief, but that after we prayed, the blood dried up immediately!

Amazing Divine Provision
My wife and I went out ministering one day with my elder sister. We were out all day. Returning towards the evening, I told my wife that when we got home, I would like to eat yam. She retorted that we needed to get home first, and I responded that I spoke because I was very hungry. As soon as we got home, my wife went to the basement, took a tuber of yam, and went into the kitchen, but before she cut the yam, we heard the doorbell ring. My wife moved towards the door, but I beat her to it. When I opened the door, I found a woman with a dish, which she took straight to the kitchen.

102

When my wife opened the dish, it was yam pottage. My wife did not have to cut the yam. We ate, thanked the woman, and my wife returned her cleaned plates. I let the woman out and locked the door.

Less than three minutes later, I heard the doorbell ring again. Thinking the woman had forgotten something, I went to open the door only to find that a man had brought another type of yam pottage. It was a special yam pottage delicacy from my own locality known as 'ikokore.' My sister, wife, and I were amazed by the kindness of God. These incidents never cease to amaze me. I learned many lessons about the character of God. Indeed, God does exceedingly, abundantly above what we ask or think. He meets our needs according to His riches in glory by Christ Jesus. He knows what we need before we ask Him. His timing is perfect. He moves people to act in our favor. He provides for those who serve Him!

Starting A Radio Network With A Cracked Phone
The Lord told a man that he should start a radio network. For four years, he had been looking for resources to start the network. In a meeting, I asked him why he had not started the network he had been talking about for the past four years. He told me that he had difficulty securing the resources that he needed. I knew that his approach was wrong, and I said, "When I was starting the ministry, the Lord told me, 'Start where you are and use what I have given you.'" I challenged him to start with what he had. He replied that he had nothing, but in his hand was a phone with a cracked screen. I encouraged him to start with the phone. Incredulously, he looked at the phone and at me, and I told him that if he would commit, the Lord would provide what he needed.

A week later, we started recording with the cracked phone. At the second recording, he came with an iPad that had a cracked screen, which someone had given to him that week. With excitement, we thanked the Lord for the iPad. I emphasized that because he committed to the work, the Lord had started building the network. Within a month, he received a gift of a new iPad. Again, we celebrated the goodness of God for progress, and he was even more motivated. His wife, who had no computer skills, was used by God to build a beautiful website for the network. One day, after we finished our recording, we prayed that the Lord would provide him with the desk and chair that he needed for the network. Driving him home, we saw a desk and chair on the curbside. They were fairly new. We stopped, knocked at the door of the house in front of which they were, to inquire if we could have them. The woman in the house said that she was just praying that the Lord would send someone who needed it to pick it up. We were excited, thanked the woman, loaded up the desk and chair, and took them to his house.

We continued meeting weekly to record and build content for the network. Other programs were added, the website was launched, and the network was fully functional. The man, having learned how God works, never ceases to teach others how God uses small and inconsequential things to do His great and mighty works. The word I received from the Lord about starting where we are and using what we have has helped many people. It is untrue that we do not have what we need to do what God wants us to do. God always starts big things small. We must open our eyes and see what God has given us to use for His will. God used a phone with a cracked screen to build a modern radio network!

Radio Ministry
At the beginning of our ministry, the Lord promised that we would have a radio ministry. I had no idea how to start it. I began visiting a church in Swansea, MA, and became friends with the pastor. His secretary called to invite me to lunch with the pastor. Before leaving home, I wrote a small note, which I put in my pocket, to discuss starting a radio ministry with him. At lunch with us were his daughter and another

member of his church. As we ate, the pastor asked, "Pastor Femi, do you love challenges?" I replied, "It depends on what challenge it is." He said that he would like me to minister on his radio program once a week. Then, I showed him the note that I had in my pocket. The Lord used him to open the door to the radio ministry without my initiating the discussion. I began ministering on his radio program on Fridays. Later, God gave us our own radio ministry in the same network. Our program was discontinued; however, when the radio station was bought by a new owner. I kept my peace because I didn't know exactly what to do next.

One day, I received an invitation to a meeting at Salem Radio in Boston, and we were offered a contract to minister on their radio station. Our radio ministry began anew. Again, we received an invitation to Wilkins Radio and expanded to South Carolina, Pennsylvania, Ohio, Jacksonville, Florida, and Mississippi. Our radio ministry is expanding. We kept receiving invitations to take on new areas. Just like the Indian ministry, the Lord gave us a radio ministry even when I didn't know how to start it.

24/7 Radio App
In the year 2022, the Lord told me that two extra radio channels were open, and two months later, Wilkins Radio offered us exactly two radio channels. In the year 2023, the Lord said that our radio ministry would be enlarged. Again, Wilkins Radio offered us four new stations later that year. In January 2024, the Lord said, *"24/7 radio is better."* Knowing that, I did not take on additional stations offered to us that year to expand our radio ministry. Instead, we decided to build an app for 24/7 radio so that people can enjoy nonstop enrichment of their souls by the word of the Lord. The Lord is involved and has been guiding this ministry step by step to accomplish His desire. From experience, I know that if we follow the counsel of the Lord, ministry will not be burdensome at all.

105

Accident Victim Healed

We were on vacation when we received news from one of our members. The stepson of the younger brother of his boss was involved in an accident, and he wanted us to pray for him. We cut short our vacation and went to the hospital to pray for the person. The Lord took control and fully restored him. Our member's boss visited me and expressed his gratitude for cutting short our vacation to pray for his brother's stepson. Being a successful businessman and desiring to give us an offering, he asked if we raised donations for our ministry, and I told him that we do not. He asked what he could do to help our ministry, and I told him that we do not solicit help. For many months, he kept asking me what he could do, and one day I told him that if the Lord wanted him to do anything, He would tell him what he should do.

Some months later, the man came to see me and, with excitement, said, "Pastor Femi, you were right. The Lord spoke to me clearly about what to do." He brought out a check from his pocket and gave it to me. It was for five thousand dollars. He also told me many things that the Lord spoke to him about his own family. The man who had never heard God speak before began hearing the voice of God, and we have remained close friends ever since.

From this experience, I was able to understand that if we give room to the Lord to use us, He would do multiple things to bless His people through us. We acted on the need of the moment just as our Lord Jesus did. When the centurion sent for Jesus Christ because of his servant, He responded, saying, "I will come and heal him." Matthew 8:7. We responded to the request without putting our own convenience above their need. We did it without any ulterior motive, and the Lord used our effort to touch the family. If we act in the will of the Lord, He will build a lasting relationship that will give us the opportunity to influence people in His way.

106

The Earth Shifted By An Earthquake

Beginning in the year 2009, the Lord began to speak to me about events that would occur in the future. Concerning the year 2010, the Lord said that He would begin to shake the world. He said that He would not shake the world to destroy it, but so that mankind may recognize Him as the sovereign God and turn to Him. He said that He would shake the world and the earth would move. I gave the message in our crossover service on December 31, 2009. Beginning in January 2010, several earthquakes began shaking the world. That year, geological reports confirmed that the 8.8 magnitude Chilean earthquake of March 3, actually moved the earth.

Clenched Fist Healed

A woman who suffered from a clenched fist for three years said that she was healed while listening to the word of God preached at an outdoor revival of the church. For the first time in three years, she was able to open her clenched fist. What a mighty God we serve. He works wonders.

AFTERWORD - Importance of Testimonies

The people who gave us the testimonies of what the Lord did in their lives helped us to know how God works. If they hadn't told us, we would not have known. Testimonies inform people of what the Lord does. They inspire faith and hope. They trigger gratitude, and they fortify our spirit when we look back on them in times of challenge. Testimonies can be reproduced. If you have any situation similar to any in this book, you can use the testimonies as a point of contact and talk to the Lord. He will answer you because, as Romans 10:11-13 says, *"Whoever believes on Him will not be put to shame. For there is no distinction between the Jew and the Greek, for the same Lord over all is rich to all that call upon Him. For whoever calls on the name of the Lord shall be saved."*

107

God Can Use You Too

In 1998, I was thrown in at the deep end because I started ministry without any knowledge or experience in a foreign land. The miraculous works of God detailed in this book were what we experienced in the course of time. They prove that the Lord Jesus Christ is real and that He indeed is the Savior. He is at work in the lives of those who believe in Him. Being born and raised in a Muslim household and not equipped with any spiritual skills, by faith I responded to His call, and over the years, He has proved the authenticity and truth of the call.

You may not know anything, but if God has called you, trust and follow Him. Let me tell you, you don't have to know anything. The One who called you knows all things. It is the responsibility of the person who wants you to do something for him to tell you what he wants you to do, because if he does not tell you, you cannot know. God also knows that if He does not tell you what you are to do for Him, you cannot know. If you study the Scriptures from Genesis to Revelation, God always tells people what He wants them to do, when, where, with what, and how.

Ministry Is To Do What God Tells You To Do

It was God who told Noah to build an ark. He gave him the dimensions, the type of wood he should use, what he would use to seal it, how many levels the ark would have, who and what would be in it - Noah, his wife, sons, their wives, animals, and food. God gave Moses the blueprint for the tabernacle in the wilderness. God told him how to gather resources for building it. He appointed those who would work on it and gave them the wisdom, knowledge, and understanding they needed by the Holy Spirit. You must study the ministry of Moses. God told Moses what he would do at every point, and he did it. The only time he acted on his own, by striking the rock instead of speaking to it as God instructed, he lost his ministry - Numbers 20:7-13. Our Lord

Jesus Christ said, *"Most assuredly, I say to you, the Son can do nothing of Himself, but what He sees the Father do; for whatever He does, the Son also does in like manner. [20] For the Father loves the Son, and shows Him all things that He Himself does; and He will show Him greater works than these, that you may marvel." John 5:19-20.*

If the Son can do nothing of Himself and needed the Father to instruct and direct Him, why should we worry that we cannot do things of ourselves? Jesus told us, *"Abide in Me, and I in you. As the branch cannot bear fruit of itself, unless it abides in the vine, neither can you, unless you abide in Me. [5] "I am the vine, you are the branches. He who abides in Me, and I in him, bears much fruit; for without Me you can do nothing." John 15:4-5.* Trusting and taking instructions from the Lord is to abide in Him. We should not jump around thinking we are fulfilling ministry. We should wait on the Lord, take instructions from Him, and do what He instructs without changing it.

I used to feel that my lack of experience was a liability in fulfilling the ministry, but now I realize it is an asset. We can only wait on the Lord to direct us since we don't know what to do. This has been a phenomenal blessing to us. If God does not instruct it, we don't do it, even if it is being done by others. At the beginning of the ministry, the Lord told me not to copy. He told me through several visions, which He later interpreted to me, that "I am the One that knows where I am taking you and the way there. You must follow Me. When I sit down, you sit. When I get up to go, you follow." He also told me that I should not be in a hurry but to keep pace with Him. He also said that I should not follow shortcuts because it would lead to a dead end and a waste of time. With this understanding, I told the church that "The longer way is shorter!"

109

We fulfill Ministry Not By Our Own Initiative

God will use us if we are willing to take instructions from His mouth - Job 22:22. If we trust the Lord with all our heart and don't lean on our own understanding but acknowledge Him in all things, He will direct our path - Proverbs 3:5. We are not called to direct our own steps. As Jeremiah 10:23 says, *"O LORD, I know the way of man is not in himself; It is not in man who walks to direct his own steps."* When we act according to our own counsel, we demote rather than promote ourselves. Jeremiah 7:23-24 says, *"But this is what I commanded them, saying, Obey My voice, and I will be your God, and you shall be My people. And walk in all the ways that I have commanded you, that it may be well with you.'* [24] *Yet they did not obey or incline their ear, but followed the counsels and the dictates of their evil hearts, and went backward and not forward.* No human wisdom or counsel can rival the wisdom and counsel of God.

OTHER BOOKS BY THE AUTHOR

From Muslim and Occultism to Bishop

God Is The Master Builder

The Work of Life

Understanding Kingdom Economy

Principles of Divine Promotion

The New Covenant Priest

You Have Been Delivered

Understanding The Purpose of God

Knowing and Fulfilling the Purpose of God

The Power of Purpose

Overcoming the Trials of Life

The Wonderful Works of God

About the Author

Femi Owoyemi was born into a Muslim family. He graduated as a Chartered Management Accountant (Prize Winner) at South West London College in 1977. He earned an MBA with distinction from the University of Lagos in 1985 and attended the Manchester Business School - Senior International Bankers Program in 1991. He is a member of the Institute of Chartered Accountants and the Institute of Management Consultants, both in Nigeria.

He was a Financial Management Consultant at KPMG. He joined First City Merchant Bank (now First City Monument Bank) in 1989 as Senior Manager and retired in the position of Deputy General Manager in 1992.

Femi Owoyemi became born again through a divine encounter in 1992. He attended the Word of Faith Bible Institute (WOFBI) - June 1996, holds an Associate degree in Theology from the Evangelical Theological College of West Africa in 2003, and a Post Graduate Diploma in Theology from the Redeemed Christian Bible College in 2003. He was awarded an honorary doctorate in Theology from the Evangelical Theological College of West Africa in 2012.

He was ordained an Evangelist in Christ Miracle Vineyard Church in 1994, Pastor in 1998, and District Superintendent (North American Missions) in 2001. He planted two branches of Christ Miracle Vineyard Church in the United States, one in Providence, RI, in 1998 and the other in Boston, MA, in 2000.

In 2010, the Lord called him to establish Kingdom Lighthouse Church in Providence, RI. He has preached extensively and held several outdoor crusades/revivals in Nigeria and the United States. He is married to Pastor Modupe Owoyemi, an attorney, and they are blessed with many children.

www.ingramcontent.com/pod-product-compliance
Lightning Source LLC
LaVergne TN
LVHW041231080426
835508LV00011B/1148